POETS AND DREAMERS

POETS AND DREAMERS

GLOBAL ICONS AND INNOVATORS: WOMEN SHAPING OUR WORLD

REDEFINING LEADERSHIP

ANNE TAMMEL

When women understand what we're truly capable of — and we unite in that knowing — there is no ceiling.

— ANNE TAMMEL

CONTENTS

THE ARCHITECTURE OF WHAT'S NEXT

I launched a leadership series because I knew something. I knew the way you know weather is coming before the sky changes — the way a woman knows the room has shifted before anyone speaks. I knew it from decades of sitting across from executives, from building authentically diverse communities, from watching what happens when people show up confident in their power and celebrate together in a different way.

What I knew was this: when women truly begin to understand what we are capable of — and when we unite and empower one another in that understanding — the results will be infinite. There is no ceiling. There is no sky high enough to contain what we achieve.

Women are not a sideline to innovation. We are not the support chorus. We are not waiting to be invited onto the stage.

We often begin the dialogue. We initiate the innovative process, do the work to actualize it, connect the people who need to find each other, cross-pollinate across industries and borders, implement what others left on the whiteboard, then make it accessible to the world. Ada Lovelace wrote the first computer program. Grace Hopper built the first compiler and gave machines the ability to understand human language. Hedy Lamarr co-invented frequency-hopping technology that became the foundation for WiFi, GPS, and Bluetooth. Stephanie Kwolek created Kevlar — five times stronger than steel. Six women programmed ENIAC, the first electronic computer, and were not credited for decades. The $8.3 billion nail care industry exists because twenty Vietnamese refugee women followed a curiosity about Tippi Hedren's manicured nails. These are not exceptions. This is the pattern.

Then we invite men onto our stage and into the center of our story. We always have. That generosity is a strength, not a weakness. But the origin is ours.

Women own 42% of all businesses in the United States. We launched 49% of new businesses in 2024 — the highest share ever recorded. Women-founded startups generate 78 cents of revenue per dollar invested, compared to 31 cents for those led by men. The data is not ambiguous: women are building the economy.

But the data also says otherwise. The International Monetary Fund projects that 40% of global jobs will be disrupted by artificial intelligence — and that women's roles will be hit hardest. The World Bank confirmed it in 2026: women hold just two-thirds of the legal rights of men. Not a single economy on earth grants women full economic equality. Only 4% of women worldwide live in countries that come close. Women-led startups still receive barely 2% of venture capital. The gap between what women build and what the world expects us to build is not closing fast enough.

This book exists because I have spent twenty-five years sitting across from leaders who are changing that.

The conversations collected here span Silicon Valley, Orange County, fourteen countries, the Vietnamese refugee story that built an $8.3 billion industry, the neuroscience of cultural intelligence, and organizational transformations that prove what is possible when the right leader enters the room. These are not theoretical discussions about leadership. They are working blueprints from founders, strategists, and innovators who have repositioned companies, rebuilt cultures, and created industries.

This is not aspiration. This is what I have created. In peer advisory circles, where CEOs bring challenges they cannot share with anyone else and leave with solid strategy. At SoCal Women in Business gatherings, where strangers leave as collaborators who built something neither could have imagined alone. And with c-suite leaders one on one, who shift their mindset and approach then walk out with a strategy to reorient their entire organization.

A CEO who sat across from me convinced her company had hit its ceiling — then left with a renewed vision, a force field map of what was driving and blocking her acceleration, then a step-by-step roadmap to scale it. A founder at first afraid to let anyone go, who adopted a leadership model that grew her venture four times over. A CEO threatened with succession — who reoriented her strategy, held her ground, and realigned the entire organization behind her leadership. An executive — most brilliant at the table — who couldn't get the room to listen, then learned to articulate her worth; the revenue and title followed. A woman with capabilities no one could see — until we built her positioning strategy. She now leads financial strategy at the billion-dollar level.

That is the work. This book holds ten conversations with leaders who are building the global business architecture of what's next.

Andy Cunningham, who positioned and scaled the greatest tech leaders of her time. Hélène Blanchette, who led across fourteen countries and is building a Cultural Intelligence Center at Chapman University that will reshape how the next generation conducts business across borders. Van Lai-DuMone, whose mother — one of twenty Vietnamese refugees — built an eight-billion-dollar industry by tapping into their innate strengths. Bonni Pomush, who transformed an organization from the inside out — moving a Glassdoor rating from 2.3 to 4.3, tripling the clients served, and shifting her culture from institution to ecosystem — in two years. Lacy Schoen, who is building an international blueprint for women in leadership. Dita Shemke, who identified the invisible barrier to the boardroom then built the structure to cross it. Mikelle Standbridge, who restored a sixteenth-century monastery in Piedmont and taught us to listen to what the silence promises. Michèle Fattal, who coaches leaders to achieve bold outcomes through visual and creative arts. And Stacie Shepard, who models effective teamwork through the instincts of the pack.

The tenth conversation is different. In it, Bonni Pomush, a transformative leader raising the vibration for humanity right here in Orange County, asks the questions of me — and for the first time in this series, I speak in my own voice about what leaders are capable of individually and collectively, what has driven me from the beginning to build and lead this movement, and what I believe is possible when we achieve the momentum we need to make this vision real.

Each of these leaders spoke generously when I invited them to share their story. Each spoke with the honesty that only comes when a leader knows she is being heard.

The book closes with Persephone.

In the myth, Persephone is taken. She is silenced. She is given a throne but not the power that comes with it. And she finds a way to rule anyway — not by force, not by permission, but by becoming something no one had imagined.

Every woman in this book has a Persephone story. Every woman reading this book has one as well.

This is one book of many volumes. There will be more.

Anne Tammel

AUTHOR'S NOTE

There is a difference between a woman waiting for permission and a leader who has decided to build.

The first asks to be accepted.

The second declares what she is building.

The transition from waiting to be included to building is the complete journey.

Once I decided to lead from my core, I stopped waiting for rooms to wake up and invite. I built my own.

The conversations in this book come from that same idea: when leaders gather in rooms built on trust rather than hierarchy, something powerful happens. People stop managing perception and start building from truth.

Poets and Dreamers is one of those rooms. It began as a place where strategy meets culture — where leaders reflect on the forces that shaped them and the ideas they are building next.

These conversations are not interviews in the usual sense. They are authentic, organic conversations about leadership, innovation, global business strategy, and the choices that shape the future of industries and economies.

The leaders in these pages are founders, strategists, innovators, and cultural architects. They have built organizations, transformed communities, and changed the direction of the industries they entered.

This book is an invitation to listen.

ACKNOWLEDGMENTS

I am grateful to the leaders, founders, strategists, and innovators who shared their perspectives in these conversations. Each of you has shaped industries and society through the organizations you built and the ideas you advanced. Your willingness to reflect openly on leadership, innovation, and the forces reshaping global business made this book possible.

My thanks also go to the many colleagues, early readers, and supporters who encouraged the development of this project as the ideas evolved.

I remain deeply grateful to the leadership communities that have grown around this work — including the leaders and members of OC CEO Collective, SoCal Women in Business, and the broader international Poets and Dreamers society. These rooms demonstrate what happens when thoughtful leaders gather in an environment built on trust, curiosity, and shared purpose.

In 2001, I founded Poets and Dreamers International — a global creative society that has grown from fewer than 200 to over 2,200 members since 2008. In 2024, I introduced

Redefining Leadership with OC CEO Collective at The Park Club, bringing a new approach to leadership to the region — built from Silicon Valley strategy, the USC approach to neuroscience, jazz and organizational dynamics, and ICF core principles. I followed by launching OC Women in Business at The Cove at UCI Beall Applied Innovation from a disparate community, pioneering the concept of Uniting and Empowering Women in Business and growing the organization 475% in less than three months.

In 2025, I expanded on OC Women in Business, launching SoCal Women in Business, then introduced the region's first leadership lunch and strategy series at The Park Club California designed for women CEOs, founders, and senior executives, as well as Global CEO Collective Peer Advisory Circles. In April 2026, we introduce Uniting and Empowering Women Worldwide with the first ever Global Women in Innovation Summit.

These communities redefine the leadership infrastructure of Orange County — a region at the center of California's $4.3 trillion economy, the world's fourth largest, where we introduce the Global Chamber Orange County connecting the region to international trade and business across six continents, and where the 2026 Economic Opportunity Report confirmed the region's most valuable asset is its people.

The conversations in this book reflect that conviction — that when leaders gather across borders, industries, and disciplines, the architecture of what's next becomes visible.

I thank the builders and leaders working across industries and around the world who continue to shape the conversation about leadership, innovation, and culture. These discussions continue in leadership circles and boardrooms where executives gather to challenge assumptions, clarify strategy, and guide the organizations they lead.

Together, they are helping redefine leadership for a new era.

Anne Tammel

BRINGING INNOVATION TO MARKET
IN CONVERSATION WITH ANDY CUNNINGHAM

Andy Cunningham shaped the technology industry's approach to positioning and messaging for more than four decades. With an English degree and a creative background in music, she built and led the premier PR firm in Silicon Valley—and for a time, the world.

Having launched the most iconic technology brands of our era, Andy's journey from trumpet performance major to Steve Jobs' trusted advisor reveals the power of creativity in technology—transforming the way innovative companies communicate value.

At the height of the Macintosh launch, Andy shaped the narrative of Silicon Valley, then carried it forward by founding Cunningham Communication, Inc. The agency brought to market the defining tech companies of its era and grew to $50 million in revenue.

Standing at the center of technology's most transformative moments—from launching the Macintosh to building a 250-person agency—she later codified her positioning methodology in *Get to Aha!*, giving innovators a framework for articulating identity, category, and purpose.

Today, she leads Cunningham Collective, where her Six Cs framework—Core, Competition, Community, Category, Context, Competence—guides leaders toward alignment between identity, strategy, and expression.

Her philosophy was not born from theory but in war rooms with Jobs, Sculley, and hundreds of CEOs navigating chaos.

My connection to Andy started out on a sunlit Willow Glen morning in the nineties. I opened the San Jose Business Journal's *Book of Lists* and learned that the top-ranked PR firm in the Valley was led by a woman—a woman with an English degree. Months later, I was hired by Cunningham Communication to build communications strategy for the Hewlett-Packard account; soon after, I was working on positioning strategy for the firm's elite clients.

From Andy, I learned competitive strategy: how to champion audacious visions, translate them so the world could understand them, then align internal cultures to achieve external success.

During those early years at Andy's firm, I also learned how to mobilize organizations to achieve what others believed impossible—and to set standards of excellence others wanted to follow.

Andy's framework still stands at the origin of my own. I carried forward what I learned from Andy's strategic methodology and cultural discipline of the Cunningham Way, later integrating both with what I learned at USC, my work as a connector and leader in Orange County, and twenty-five years advising leaders—then building my own architecture.

From Andy, I also learned another rare skill. To practice integrity and do so relentlessly. Integrity means honoring your core value system, especially when tested in the toughest moments—like the moment when Steve Jobs is about to make a major mistake in front of the press and you hold your ground to protect him. Steve Jobs was famous throughout the Bay Area for listening to nobody. Yet when it came to Andy, he listened. And he learned.

In this conversation, Andy and I returned to the stories behind the brands, the philosophy beneath the work, and the leadership approach it took to guide some of Silicon Valley's most consequential figures. We traced the history and intention behind her philosophy, the chaos of the dot-com bust, the inner world and elusive power of Steve Jobs, and the role of AI and ethics in today's marketing landscape.

For Andy, the message has always been clear: align with your DNA—or disappear.

ANNE TAMMEL

Andy, I appreciate this conversation. As a child of Silicon Valley, I've watched it evolve all around me and it seems the history is getting a bit lost.

ANDY CUNNINGHAM

It's great to reconnect. My real dream is to write a book or do a documentary on the Coming of Age of Silicon Valley. All these people are starting to die so I need to do it soon.

TAMMEL

I hope you do. When I worked at Cunningham, there was a woman helping with your book, and I said, "I wish I could be working on Andy's book." And I recently said to my son, "Every syllable, every mark of punctuation in her book belongs there." –which is so true to your style.

CUNNINGHAM

Thank you for noticing. I remember we copy edited that until the cows came home.

TAMMEL

The outcome speaks for itself. I was so impressed in my twenties to find a woman with an English degree running the top tech PR firm in Silicon Valley.

CUNNINGHAM

I am a person who has always had extreme respect and awe for technology. Always. I was very good with science, but I dropped out of math at the beginning of my sophomore year in high school. So therefore I couldn't be involved really in technology as doing it myself. But what I am driven to do, and what my personal mission in life is, is to bring innovation to market. And that is what I do.

TAMMEL

And what a track record. It actually came up last night at USC—Apple's 1984 ad. So I looked it up and said, "That's Andy Cunningham's history." Can you share how you became involved with Steve Jobs and the launch of the Mac?

CUNNINGHAM

I was working at Burson-Marsteller in Chicago. They were one of the largest at the time, and I was working in what they called their technical group, which meant the accounts I was serving were B2B. They were kind of technical back in the early, early 80s, and our company started to see the potential in Silicon Valley to expand and build an office there. They did build an office. A friend of mine went to work there, and he kept sending me notes through interoffice mail: "Andy, you would just die here. This is the most fabulous place on earth. Please consider coming and working in our office."

So I got my boss to give me a couple of days off to fly out to California—because I was living in Chicago—and to meet with the guy running the office there. I did, and I cannot tell you—I found him to be arrogant, chauvinistic, basically kind of an ass. I said to myself at the end of the meeting, "Oh my God, I don't think I can work for this guy, as much as I want to be here."

I had a few more hours left in the day, and I started randomly calling PR firms. I looked them up in the phone book and found a handful. So I started calling and said, "I happen to be in town. I'm from Burson-Marsteller in Chicago. I'm looking to move to Silicon Valley. Do you have any time today?"

By the end of the day, I had meetings with three different agencies. The last one of the day was Regis McKenna. I was interviewing with Regis, and at the end of the interview, he said to me, "I'd like to offer you a job running the Apple account for the launch of their next computer, which is Macintosh." I'm like, "Oh my God, I can't believe this." And so I said, "Yes, I'll take it."

That's how I wound up leaving Burson-Marsteller. That's how I wound up working with Apple.

I started at Regis about a month later. There was one woman left at Regis McKenna who was working on the Apple account. The rest of the team had quit. They had just launched the Lisa computer, which was a giant failure. They were all kind of down and depressed, and they left.

So it was just this one young woman named Jane Anderson. She and I formed a team together, and we wrote the whole launch plan. We did the whole thing pretty much alone, working very closely with Steve and also their head of marketing at Apple, a guy named Mike Murray, who was fabulous.

We went to work at Apple every day. It was an incredible experience, and that's how I got to know Steve Jobs.

We ended up growing the account team, adding a few more people to the group. But at the end of the day, how it sort of shook out was: my personality was more suited to deal with Steve on a day-to-day basis, and Jane's personality was more suited to deal with John Sculley, who was the CEO at the time. That's kind of how we divided and conquered the world of the Apple account.

So I worked very, very closely with Steve.

Then when Steve got fired from Apple, he called me about ten days later and said, "I'm starting a new company, and I'm having a press conference at my house right now. Can you come? Can you come over and help?"

So I went over to his house in Woodside. There were 50 or so business press journalists milling around the front yard. I got through them and went inside the house. True to legend, there wasn't a stick of furniture in the house. He and seven other people were sitting on the floor in the kitchen. I was standing; they were all seated. The person right next to Steve was his lawyer, but everybody else were people I knew really well from Apple.

He looked up at me and said, "I'm having a press conference in a few minutes. I'm going to announce to the world that I'm starting a new company. We're going to call it NeXT. I'm taking these people from Apple. Oh, and by the way, I'm going to tell everybody what an asshole John Sculley is."

I looked at him—my mouth dropped open. Finally, I said, "You can't do that. You can't have a press conference. You have nothing to announce. You haven't even fully left Apple. These people are still Apple employees. You just can't do it. It's the wrong thing to do."

He looked up at me, thought for a minute, and said, "Okay, I won't do it. But you have to go out there and get rid of everybody."

So I went out and told everybody the truth. I said, "Look, he's been gone for ten days. He wants to start another company. He'll do it, but there's no company, no product, nothing to announce. You already know that he has left Apple. I promise you—when there's something to talk about, I will reach out to each and every one of you."

They mumbled and grumbled, but they all left peacefully.

That was how I got hooked up with Steve—even more intimately than when I was working with him at Regis McKenna.

TAMMEL

No matter what anyone says about Steve, I will always defend him. He gave so much to us.

CUNNINGHAM

You should take a look at the movie called *Steve Jobs*. Aaron Sorkin is the writer. There's been many Steve Jobs movies. This is the most recent one, simply called *Steve Jobs*. It was modeled on the biography of Steve Jobs that Walter Isaacson wrote. I'm a character in the movie, so it shows my relationship with Steve very well. I helped Walter with the biography, so I'm in the biography as well.

TAMMEL

It sounds like you had a positive relationship with him, and I want the world to know him in that way.

CUNNINGHAM

I had as good a relationship as anybody can have. He had a person who ran strategy for him, another woman named Joanna Hoffman. She's the other star, played by Kate Winslet in the movie. She's opposite Michael Fassbender, who played Steve Jobs. She really had a very close relationship with Steve, much closer than mine. But I did get along pretty well with him.

If you could add value to his mission in life, he valued you. He didn't think he knew everything. He did know a lot of things, but there were a lot of things he didn't know.

He wasn't a programmer. He wasn't a hardware designer. He wasn't a marketing person. So he would take from you what would help his mission and discard the rest.

So we all felt—all of us, there were about a hundred of us involved in the Macintosh—and we all felt we were changing the world. And he gave us that gift of making us feel that way. And we would have done anything for him— pretty much anything.

TAMMEL

And you did change the world.

CUNNINGHAM

It's cool to be part of something that did change the world.

TAMMEL

I know he valued creativity, and I think it's fascinating that we come to this business as creative spirits to contribute what we do. It's pivotal. I'd love to hear about your background as a creative person.

CUNNINGHAM

I started college as a performance major in music—I played the trumpet. Every minute of every day was taken up playing my horn. I was playing trumpet ten hours a day, all classical music.

I've always been an artist in that sort of way. I also took many years of dance. It was an emotional expression I really enjoyed. So when I got to college as a music major, I saw myself as a creative.

I was never going to be a science major; I didn't have the math. But I was a damn good trumpet player. I was good enough to get in with a great audition, but I wanted to be in a major symphony. There are maybe twelve of those jobs in the world.

So I asked myself, "What else do I do well?" I write well. I dropped out of the music school and got accepted into the creative writing program in the Department of English at Northwestern.

TAMMEL

As a writer and creator, there is this myth that with technology, you don't really understand the conversation. And yet, you're the woman driving the conversation. You're creating the messages that go out.

CUNNINGHAM

Yes, exactly. These people—these brilliant engineers—they don't know how to talk about what they're doing. When I started my own firm after I left Regis McKenna, I realized I had a problem. I was doing PR, taking these engineers out to the *New York Times* and *Wall Street Journal*, and when they opened their mouths, it was bad. All wrong. They didn't understand how to talk about strategy, about why they mattered, or who they were.

If I was going to help them bring innovation to market, people had to understand what they were doing. And they couldn't talk to normal people. That's what started me on the path of what I really do now—positioning and messaging, which is my passion.

It all started with trying to help a CEO explain his company to the *New York Times*—and failing.

TAMMEL

Can we hear about how your journey evolved after that? I came into the picture in the mid-90s at Cunningham.

CUNNINGHAM

I started my company after Steve got fired. At Regis McKenna, I was on the wrong side of the political equation —sidelined with Steve, which was not a great place to be.

So I figured it was a good time to start my own firm. Regis was wonderful about it. He let me use the office, the computers, the photocopiers. He was fabulous.

After that interaction with Steve at his house, he wanted to work with me. It was just me at the time, but I hired a couple of people early on. Once I had Steve Jobs as a client, it was easy to get everyone else. That's how I became the biggest firm in Silicon Valley—probably the country at that time.

When you've done work for Steve, you have credibility. I may not have earned all of it, but I got it, and I used it. I built a relatively large agency. When I sold the firm, we had 250 people and were doing $50 million in revenue.

The reason I sold it—after about 15 years—was Motorola. They were a very big client, and the head of marketing, Rusty Bush, made it clear they needed an international PR firm. We had one office in London and nothing else internationally. He let me know we probably wouldn't keep the account without that global capability. I'd had that business for a long time—John Sculley helped me get it, actually.

So I hired a banker, went through the process, and sold to a company called Citigate. I liked the people, and our firm would be the biggest in their portfolio. But 60 days later, the dot-com bubble burst. Silicon Valley turned into what we called "see-through buildings." My business imploded. I had to fire people every week. I let go of 235 out of 250 people. It was awful.

TAMMEL

That's heavy.

CUNNINGHAM

After I lived out my contract with Citigate, I negotiated a deal to buy back the strategy division. I couldn't do PR anymore because of a non-compete, but I started another agency to do brand strategy. I brought over about eight people from Cunningham and we created a firm called CXO Communication. Kathleen Boden, my primary partner, still runs it out of Boston today. They do a lot of Marcom work.

After eight years of that, I was tired. I never really recovered from the implosion. So I took a job as a CMO at a company run by a narcissistic sociopath. After a year, I couldn't do it anymore.

That's when I started the company I have today. It's the part of the marketing equation I really love. I developed a methodology—it's in my book—that I use to help people get to what I call "Aha." I help them figure out how to talk about who they are, why they matter in a compelling way, and how to differentiate.

This work takes many forms. Sometimes it's a day of consulting. Sometimes it's a six-month project. But generally, I follow that methodology—and it works. One hundred percent of the time.

TAMMEL

Can you describe the methodology?

CUNNINGHAM

I call it the "Six C's of Positioning." These are lenses we use to look at the market.

We do research to understand the company through these lenses:

Core – This is my original concept: companies fall into one of three DNA types—Mothers, Mechanics, and Missionaries. If you don't understand your core, you'll make huge mistakes with your marketing, positioning, and go-to-market strategy.

Competition – Classic analysis, but still crucial. We study how competitors position themselves.

Community – This includes partners, customers, and influencers. We do a full study of the company's ecosystem.

Category – I've realized how strategic this is. You don't leave category definition to Gartner or Forrester. It's a huge part of the conversation.

Context – Context is everything. It defines who you are and why you matter. If you don't understand the contextual environment, you won't succeed in it.

Competence – What is the company truly great at? What is its superpower?

We take all of this and create a detailed report. Then we hold a workshop—usually three eight-hour sessions. This is where we build what I call the "Message Architecture."

The Message Architecture has four parts:

- North Star

- Strategy

- Brand Expression

- Ownable Brand Concept

There are 28 elements total—each one a tile in the mosaic of the company's identity. We spend time on each tile until the team reaches what I call "Aha"—clarity and conviction.

After that, we write a narrative—usually a page and a half—that weaves all 28 elements together. Once that's perfected, the company has everything it needs to build any communication asset: videos, websites, sales pitches, funding decks. It becomes the blueprint not just for marketing, but for product strategy and business alignment.

It defines who you are and why you matter.

TAMMEL

And that's different from executing it, right?

One part is creating the strategy, and then actually executing it is different. And it's fascinating that it works 100% of the time.

CUNNINGHAM

We've never had a client say, "You didn't get us to Aha." It's a process and a framework. I tell people: "If you trust the process, you'll get to Aha." My daughter works with me. When she first joined, she had the same doubts as everyone else. I told her, "Just do the process. Trust it." And it worked. It always does.

Now I don't have 250 people to execute all the work that comes after. But I can help manage it, point clients to partners, or we'll do a little bit of writing for them, because that's often the hardest part. We do a lot of funding decks because so many companies are trying to raise money and they can't tell their story. So we take the Message Architecture, use it as the foundation, and create a funding deck.

Since the George Floyd movement and the pandemic, companies have started to look at their values. They're refreshing them or starting from scratch, creating entirely new sets. We built a framework for that as well.

I have a strong belief: values drive behavior, behavior drives culture, and culture is brand. It starts with values. If you don't have any, it's very hard to build a brand because that chain breaks. We've been guiding a lot of companies through that "values" work, alongside positioning. It's a separate framework.

TAMMEL

So in the context of your words, "values drive behavior, behavior drives culture, and culture is brand", can we understand what culture is to you?

CUNNINGHAM

There's nothing more important in a company than its culture, because it drives behavior. It's everything. It has to be a thoughtful process. You can't just start a company and let everyone do whatever the hell they want. There have to be norms.

You remember at Cunningham—and you mentioned this earlier about copy editing—every punctuation mark mattered. That was part of our culture. Anyone in the company could pick up a document, find a mistake, and— even if it was from someone six levels above—point it out. And that person would say, "Thank you." That was our culture. Quality.

We created "The Cunningham Way." I still have it on my wall. It defined how we behaved. That was the culture I wanted to build.

Other people want different things. I wanted people who thought on their own, played a role in the industry, and believed in technology. That's what's in The Cunningham Way. And that's what we created. We had a very, very special group of people.

TAMMEL

Yes, absolutely. And the leader really sets the tone—for everyone in the organization, for everyone coming in, even in hiring. And for all the clients they serve, all the potential clients. That drives your culture. Culture is such a critical element of the leader's vision—it carries through everything.

In one of your talks, you said: "You come up with your message then infect it into absolutely everything." And that ultimately comes from the leader. It makes its way through the culture, then it makes its way everywhere.

CUNNINGHAM

When you teach your children a value system, and you live that value system as an example, it becomes the way you manage their lives. They can go out and make decisions on their own that are consistent with those values. You don't worry about it. Of course, they'll make mistakes—but basically, you've given them a framework for living.

That's exactly what happens in a company. You have to give people a framework for living inside the company. Otherwise, you end up with random, chaotic behavior that doesn't align.

I wrote about this in my book. I once talked to the founder and CEO of Digital Equipment Corporation—remember DEC? They were a mini-computer company out of Boston. Huge at the time. He said, "People see us as this giant behemoth, like a warship coming at them—unstoppable, unbeatable. But underneath the waterline of that warship are a thousand canoes, each paddling in different directions, bumping into each other." And if we could only solve that, he said, the power would be off the charts.

So it's all about alignment. Alignment is everything.

Everything we do for clients starts with understanding who they are at the core—so everything else can align with that.

Again, as a parent, you know this: if you have a child with enormous musical talent—say they're playing the violin at six like Stravinsky—you don't say at ten, "Okay, no more violin, now you're going to play soccer." You'd wind up with an unhappy kid who can't play soccer.

You don't do that—it's against their DNA. As a parent, you align what you ask the child to do with what they're already good at. You don't force them into something uncomfortable.

Same with a company. You want the company to do things aligned with who it is. Align with your core, your identity, how you talk about yourself. Align how people behave, align your values.

It's all alignment. Even with a bad idea.

TAMMEL

It's fascinating how alignment can drive the success of a company—sometimes more than the original idea itself. I've seen so many companies fail with the best idea. You can have the best idea and best strategy, but if you can't align the culture, how are you going to bring it?

CUNNINGHAM

Exactly. It all has to be aligned.

That's what leadership is all about. Creating alignment—that's the only thing you have to do as a leader.

A lot of companies don't fully understand that. You can have a bad idea and still be successful—if everybody is aligned and moving in one direction. But a good idea with alignment? That's magic. That's a beautiful thing.

TAMMEL

Are you able to share examples?

CUNNINGHAM

I'll give you a beautiful idea that never went anywhere—because it didn't have alignment. It was a company called General Magic. They were a group of people from Apple who left to start something...they had a great idea. Really great. Super clever. And they had tons of money.

But they couldn't execute. They didn't have alignment.

Another one—I actually worked with them. When Paul Allen left Microsoft, he formed a company called Asymetrix. They were a big client of mine in the early Cunningham days. I spent a lot of time with Paul. And again, they had a ton of money. But no alignment around the product. So it didn't work.

Great ideas that didn't come to fruition because there was no alignment.

TAMMEL

Your framework is a cautionary tale for leaders.

They may have an incredible idea—or not even know if it's great—but if they come to you and build that mosaic, trust the process, they might still succeed.

CUNNINGHAM

Over the course of my career, I've worked with thousands of companies. So many of them are just incremental improvements on what's already out there.

Take CRM. Salesforce basically created the market, right? They're the 800-pound gorilla. Yet we've worked with two companies in the last couple of years building another CRM system. Why? Why?

But they made that choice. Now they're competing with Salesforce. How do you win against that?

One company decided their strategy would be: we're going to be much cheaper. Just cheaper. And they are still existing today, as a result. So that's great. But it's hard.

Back when you and I were at Cunningham, there were a couple hundred tech products. Now, in the Martech world alone, there are more than 10,000. HR? Another 15,000. Financial services? Another 10,000.

Differentiation is nearly impossible now. So you have to think creatively. Go back to your earlier comment—you've got to identify your special sauce.

Because when 8,000 other products are doing similar things, it's tough.

TAMMEL

Going back to that company that decided to be cheaper— I've seen tech change so much. Not always for the better. New entrants say, "We'll do it for half" and gain market share—but they lose the essence.

CUNNINGHAM

Exactly. And sometimes companies just pick really hard problems. Just super difficult challenges.

I spent a couple of years working with a company called Groq—not Elon Musk's Grok, but the semiconductor company. The founder is a genius at building semiconductors. Truly. But he chose a very hard path. He's building the next wave of chips—post-NVIDIA. That's no easy task.

It's much easier to build a gas station or something people want every day.

Anyway, we're in a phase now where technology development—especially AI—is about to change everything we know. Everything we've operated with over the last 40 years is shifting. Applications won't even exist in a couple of years. We'll have agents doing everything.

And companies still developing yesterday's stuff? They'll become irrelevant.

It's a tough challenge. And it's why most companies die. Remember the BUNCH? That old group of computer companies—Burroughs, Unisys, NCR?

Gone. Dead. Kodak too. Not part of the BUNCH, but same fate.

What happens is this: if you're using a technology, it gets disrupted—sooner or later. And you have a choice. Disrupt yourself, or get disrupted by the market. Most companies die.

When a new technology enters the fray, it changes everything. Personal computers changed everything.

Semiconductors. The internet. And now AI. These things come in, grab companies by the cojones, and destroy them.

We're going to see a lot of destruction in this market.

That's why the big hyperscalers are working so hard to get ahead of AI—because they have to.

TAMMEL

Do you see that shift impacting the kind of work you do?

CUNNINGHAM

What I do—like me, personally—I think the magical answer for the future is not AI taking over but AI augmenting and going alongside humans. Sure, there are certain things AI will replace, just like automation replaced factory workers. There's always a level of jobs that go away. But people in creative fields, I believe, can be augmented with AI, not replaced.

Although, that said, the whole world of graphic design is completely being disrupted right now by AI. But you still need a creative person to supervise it, prompt it, guide it— so it's not like graphic design is going away for humans. We just have these great assistants now that can do things a 22-year-old college grad could do—but much faster.

As a sidebar, I was working with a company in San Francisco—we did their values and their new positioning. They wanted something to physically express their values, more than just posters on the wall. I went on to Gemini Image—an image creator—and created exactly what I wanted them to build. It expressed my idea so perfectly and so quickly that they now want to build one in each office. I'm not even a designer. So yes, AI will take away some jobs, but mostly, I think it will make us better.

I believe it's people who make technology evil, not the technology itself. There are a lot of people using tech today for evil, yes.

TAMMEL

Yes. And how do we bring back that original intention—human creativity, the original spirit behind Silicon Valley? How do we keep that intention alive in our culture and our use of technology?

CUNNINGHAM

I think we just have better help now. If you're building a SWOT analysis with AI, the way you prompt it determines what it generates—and what you do with it afterward defines its utility.

You don't just take what ChatGPT gives and turn it in like an assignment. We have better agents around us, making us better at what we do. You can rarely just take something AI produces and go with it. I look at it like having a really smart 21-year-old next to me—someone who can research anything but doesn't yet have experience or deep creativity.

TAMMEL

That's a great analogy. You're constantly teaching it.

CUNNINGHAM

You're constantly teaching it, and it really wants to help—but it doesn't have experience.

TAMMEL

I noticed you're working on a second book. Can we hear more about that and what's next for you?

CUNNINGHAM

I really want to write the sequel to *Get to Aha!*, which I'm calling *Activating Aha*. Once you have this great idea, how do you bring it to life? I developed a framework for that. I've already done some case studies.

TAMMEL

I look forward to your second book. I also noticed you'll go into companies, or they can take a course?

CUNNINGHAM

I've taught this at several universities—USC, Carnegie Mellon. At CMU, I go about three or four times a year. I can teach people how to do it in about an hour and a half. Sometimes, especially with small companies that don't have much budget, I'll go in and just teach their marketing team in a half-day session. I just walk them through the process and tell them: trust the process. It's better if I lead them through it, but it takes time and money. Sometimes they don't have that. So the cheapest way to do it? Read the book and just do it yourself.

TAMMEL

And the book will walk them through?

CUNNINGHAM

You can do it if you read the book. Of course, there's more benefit when I lead it. You know this because you consult—being an outside person gives you credibility you don't have once you take the job inside. Overnight, that credibility disappears. So I bring to the table lots of examples, lots of experience. That's what people learn from: examples.

When we do the workshop, we explain every concept with numerous examples—real companies like Nike, Patagonia—so they can see how it works in the real world.

I do this with many universities, but my favorite experience was USC. The students were optimistic, engaged, full of personality—and gumption. They were on the edge of their seats, ready to ask questions.

TAMMEL

I'll connect you. I love USC and I believe in what you bring.

In Southern California, many leaders haven't been exposed to this level of strategic thinking. At times, I still feel like a stranger—an intellectual writer from San Jose speaking a different language.

I'll sit in a CEO roundtable and talk about strategy the way we did at Cunningham—and the reaction is, *What is this? Where did this come from?*

That's what led me back to my roots—asking:

What did I learn at Cunningham?

What have I invented myself?

What have I created beyond that?

Most people here don't fully see what you bring—they don't understand it.

CUNNINGHAM

That's very kind of you to say. I really appreciate it.

Thank you for being part of our merry band.

CURIOSITY AND COURAGE IN THE WORKPLACE
IN CONVERSATION WITH VAN LAI-DUMONE

Van and I were introduced through Eric Bing, a prominent Southern California CFO, then weeks later through yet another CFO, Gary Lu, who texted Van explaining we needed to meet.

I was in the middle of launching our *Redefining Leadership* Lunch at The Park Club when I read Van's words about her mother—a Vietnamese refugee who helped build what became an eight-billion-dollar industry.

Then I started to see the connection.

This connection began long before we met, when Van Lai-DuMone's mother, shortly after arriving in America, met Tippi Hedren and, as one of 20 women refugees, tapped into their innate strengths to build what would become an $8.3 billion industry, carried forward today by Tam Nguyen and Linh Nguyen through Advance Beauty College–that continues to benefit women and men through successful careers. In the 1970s and 80s, my mother, a changemaker and policy writer for Santa Clara County, worked tirelessly outside her demanding day job–while raising five children– to help Vietnamese refugees in San Jose advance on their leadership paths and build thriving businesses. She knew that empowering promising leaders meant building greater societies; this society later became known as Silicon Valley.

Having grown up in San Jose then later moving to Orange County, home to the largest Vietnamese community outside of Vietnam, I have been innately aware of the power of this community my entire life—the resilience, intellectual curiosity, creative approach to business, and the generosity. There is so much love in this community.

When Van and I came together, it was like two powerhouse forces—like our mothers finally meeting and carrying forward this history together. Van's mother was a refugee who built something from nothing but innate strengths and the power of relationships. My mother tapped into those same instincts to empower leaders and build a community from what many saw as nothing, or an ending, or an enemy. Now we stand together, two daughters carrying forward what our mothers started.

My mother used to say that she was the "alpha" and I am the "omega." I never understood quite what that meant but it now translates to something like the "realization of a dream". What an honor that Van and I are both now able to carry forward what each of our mothers worked so hard to create from nothing but hard work, optimism, relationship-building, intelligent foresight—and most of all, a genuine need to advance society for all humankind.

ANNE TAMMEL

Van, I've found that the most powerful leadership stories never begin in a boardroom. They're born from moments when someone has to lead with nothing but instinct and courage—no title, no safety net, no time to think. I think that's where your story begins. Can we start with 1975. The Fall of Saigon. Your family's escape. How you arrived at Hope Village.

VAN LAI-DUMONE

My father was a lieutenant colonel in the South Vietnamese Air Force, and we lived on Tân Sơn Nhất Air Base in Saigon. On April 29th, 1975—the day Saigon fell to the Communist Party—my dad rushed home to my mom and said, we need to leave right now.

They packed one suitcase. My aunt, who was fourteen at the time, happened to be spending the night, and my grandfather on my dad's side lived with us. My dad had a brand new Jeep. He put us all in and tried to drive it to the embassy. It wouldn't start.

If you look at the history now, you know that everyone tried to get out at the embassy. If we had made it there, we would never have survived. We never would have been able to get out. So somehow that brand new Jeep wouldn't start.

As we stood there trying to figure a way out, two other Jeeps drove by—his subordinates. They said there are two cargo planes left on the Air Force base. Let's get you and your family on there.

My dad was carrying my grandfather. My mom was carrying my brother. My aunt had my sister. And one of my dad's soldiers was carrying me—and put me on the wrong airplane. I was separated from my parents for a while. My brother passed out on the plane. It was a treacherous situation.

We ended up landing on an island right off of Vietnam. From there, my dad and other leaders in the Air Force found other airplanes that had more fuel and were able to get us to Guam. Once we were at Guam, the U.S. military was able to help us. Our first home in the United States was at Camp Pendleton Marine Base in San Diego, where servicemen and women for the first time in U.S. history housed refugees. We stayed there for a few months and then my family was transferred to a refugee integration center in Northern California. That was Hope Village.

TAMMEL

The Jeep that wouldn't start. Being placed on the wrong airplane. Your brother losing consciousness. And yet here you are. That pattern—the moment of greatest vulnerability becoming the moment of greatest transformation—I have seen it in every leader who has ever done something that mattered. Something breaks, and what emerges is stronger than what came before. What happened next at Hope Village? Your mother was one of twenty Vietnamese refugee women who noticed Tippi Hedren's long red manicured nails. How did following a simple curiosity about nail polish lead to an eight billion dollar industry?

LAI-DUMONE

It was at Hope Village where my mom met Tippi Hedren, a Hollywood movie star who volunteered at the camp. Tippi got there and looked at the women and said, we need to find these women a career for this new country. So she set up a typing and sewing program—those were careers that were fairly easy to learn and get into at the time. Twenty women signed up, including my mom.

As they were typing and sewing, Tippi would walk around the room encouraging them. And that's when they noticed something that caught their curiosity—something different than typing and sewing. They were curious about Tippi's long red manicured nails.

Now, imagine being a Hollywood movie star, so busy. She's already created this entire program for them. She could have easily said, thank you for noticing, but keep typing. But instead of doing that, she paused and she paid attention to their curiosity. And in that pause, they were all able to ask powerful questions—like, what if? How might we become licensed manicurists?

The first small step Tippi took was to ask her local manicurist in Los Angeles, Dusty Coots Butera, to come up and teach my mom and her friends how to do a basic manicure. Weekend after weekend, that's who would come up and share what she knew. And they loved it. They were good at it. But it didn't make them licensed manicurists.

They could have stopped there. They didn't have money to go to school. Most of them didn't speak English. But rather than focusing on the challenges, they focused on the opportunity and the possibility that came with that curiosity.

Tippi went to the local beauty school—Citrus Heights Beauty College—and asked the owners if they would be willing to take on these women as students. They said yes. After four hundred hours of schooling and ten weeks, my mom and all her friends passed their manicure practicum and written tests in English. That made them the first twenty licensed Vietnamese manicurists in the United States.

The months went on and all the families from Hope Village were sponsored by churches and families and organizations around the country. My family was sponsored by a church in Santa Monica, so we moved to a little two-bedroom apartment. Tippi came to our apartment, took my mom around to find her first job, and they found it at Beau Jacques Beauty Salon.

It was there that my mom's best friend from high school, Kien Nguyen, and her husband Tam came to visit one day with their children. From that visit, Kien and Tam decided to go into the industry themselves. They got their manicure license, opened their own salon, and then in 1987 they opened Advanced Beauty College in Garden Grove—with the intention of helping other Vietnamese refugees and immigrants find a career in this country. Since 1987, they have licensed and trained over fifty thousand manicurists.

The manicure industry today is worth 8.3 billion dollars, possibly more, and it is dominated by Vietnamese Americans. Because of this story.

TAMMEL

Your mother's story was always extraordinary—she just hadn't yet claimed it as her own. I think about how early on in my career, Andy Cunningham taught me positioning is never about inventing something that isn't there. It's actually about finding what is already true then giving it language, giving it a stage. When you saw her celebrated at the Vietnamese American Nail Association event, something shifted. What was that moment?

LAI-DUMONE

This was in 2019. I had been running my business for several years, and I really wanted to do a TEDx talk around creativity and curiosity. But there's that voice in your head that says, who am I to? Someone has done that already. So that voice stopped me.

Then I attended this Vietnamese American Nail Association event where my mom, Tippi Hedren, and the other women were being celebrated for trailblazing the Vietnamese manicure industry. And when I saw my mom on stage, I thought to myself—this is my story. Who else can tell this story?

About two weeks later, I was on LinkedIn and I saw a woman I'd met at a conference several years prior post that she was producing a TEDx talk in Anaheim—the same city I saw my mom celebrated in. Her theme was TEDxWomen: Mission of Mavericks. They had all their speakers, all they were looking for was people to buy tickets.

So I bought a ticket. And I walked away from my computer and was doing something in the kitchen. And there it was —that curiosity tapping me on the shoulder. Why don't you speak on that stage? So I paid attention to that curiosity, just like my mom and her friends paid attention to theirs. I went back to the computer and emailed Erica Morrison and said, I know you have all your speakers lined up, but here's my story.

A little while later, I got an email back: We would love for you to tell your story on our stage.

As I was writing the talk, the feedback I kept getting was— it's an amazing story, but what is the through line? What is the idea worth spreading? And that's when I came up with the framework. This is a story about the power of following curiosity. Pausing and paying attention to the ideas that tap us on the shoulder. Asking powerful questions—what if? How might we? And then taking one small step forward. You don't have to know what the second or third steps are. All my mom and Tippi and her friends did was take one small step at a time. They had no idea this would grow into an 8.3 billion dollar industry.

TAMMEL

What did your mother teach you about turning constraint into possibility—about taking what looks like the end and making it the beginning?

LAI-DUMONE

My mom has always been a very positive person in terms of looking at situations and being able to turn them into something positive. I think that's just the way she's had to do it her whole life. She grew up without a lot of money. She was the oldest daughter of nine children. She always had to find solutions.

So growing up, that's what I saw. When I talk about curiosity and creativity, that's what I saw her doing out of necessity. When something would go wrong, she would get curious, then she would get creative, then she would take action. And the work I do today, bringing creative problem solving and curiosity into organizations, was truly born of watching what my mom had to do out of necessity every day.

She taught me a lot about the human spirit and the human capacity for change and growth. When something looks like the end, or you're facing a challenge or a constraint, it doesn't mean that's where things stop. Constraints actually offer a really great place for creativity and curiosity to flourish.

TAMMEL

I still stand back in awe of both of our mothers. My mother was in San Jose advocating for change, writing policies for the county, and spending her personal time empowering Vietnamese refugees to advance on their paths, launch businesses of their own, and achieve their dreams. Nobody asked her to do this. She was busy raising five children. But she also had the innate ability to spot a true leader, and she knew what kind of society was possible when great leaders are empowered.

Meanwhile, your mother—across the Bay Area—was creating an industry in response to some of the most difficult challenges a human can face. And neither knew the other existed?

LAI-DUMONE

Our mothers were living these parallel lives, but very different. My mom was tapping into strengths of resilience, of determination—out of necessity. She had no other choice but to survive and to thrive and create a life for her children. In Vietnam, my mom was a school teacher, but when she married my father, who was a lieutenant colonel in the South Vietnamese Air Force, she was a stay-at-home mom. She had a nanny for each child. She had a very good life. And then when we came over here and literally her whole life fell apart, she had to completely switch and be someone she had never been.

And then your mom—your mom was a woman who had a full-time job, she had children, and she made the choice to help others. She saw people in need and she chose to help.

In terms of parallels, I believe there is a theme of resilience, a theme of compassion, a theme of knowing what's right and wrong and doing good in the world. That is a common theme between both our moms but on different sides. My mom had to. Your mom chose to.

I was so young, back in the seventies. My dad was definitely—we lived in a patriarchal household. I saw my mom blossom over the years from a very quiet, obedient wife to a woman who owned her own business, spoke up for herself, raised her children, made friends, and really came out of her shell.

Because of both our mothers' examples, we get to do the things we're doing today. Be women in leadership. Lead with our strengths. Lead with authenticity. Without quite the concern that our moms had. Really leaning into our strengths and just being able to be authentically who we are.

TAMMEL

When we first connected, I shared my story—which was very personal. The unique floral arrangements that filled my mother's home, the beautiful restaurants and celebrations we were invited to on the most important days, and friendships that lasted from the time I was twelve years old, then my closest Vietnamese friends flying down for my wedding. When I finished explaining that, you said: "Your connection to the Vietnamese community is what makes it such a great story."

LAI-DUMONE

I just think this is the way the universe works, bringing people into our lives who are meant to be here.

We were young children when our parents were going through these parallel lives. Your mom was helping Vietnamese refugees. My family was a Vietnamese refugee. And for us to come together now and work together, collaborate, help leaders—it is truly serendipitous.

I almost feel like it has already been written. We were meant to meet. We were meant to work together. Our moms were building this future for us. My mom being a trailblazer in the Vietnamese manicure industry–and your mom helping Vietnamese refugees build businesses. They had no idea they were running these parallel lives that led us to meeting and continuing their legacies.

TAMMEL

This is the reason I asked you to be our inaugural keynote at our SoCal Women in Business Leadership Lunch. It almost felt like our mothers were finally meeting—like what they both started was finally reaching a destination.

You've talked about one woman committing to empowering other women and the possibilities that creates.

What does it look like when more women make that commitment?

LAI-DUMONE

Two women coming together with a commitment to empower other women is exponential.

I'm a believer that women particularly have this power of collaboration, of building community. When we come together for a common goal—empowering other women to step into their identities, to step into leadership roles, and to use their voice—it really can change the world.

I think about Tippi. One woman willing to empower twenty women simply to gain a career so they could feed their families. And look what that led to. Not just an 8.3 billion dollar industry—think about the thousands of families, the lives that were changed. When women come together to empower other women, not only do those other women thrive—entire communities thrive.

TAMMEL

Van, one of the things I have learned sitting across from leaders, founders, and Olympic athletes is that the title tells very little about the actual person. The real question is always: do people genuinely want to follow them? What makes someone a leader, in your view?

LAI-DUMONE

I've always thought of a leader as someone that other people want to follow, because they are setting a good example and showing this concept of trust. When I think of trust, I think of the work of Frances Frei and Anne Morriss and their work, Begin with Trust. They talk about the trust triangle—that people need to see from you that you are authentic, that you are empathetic, and that you are logical. When leaders can show those three things consistently, people can trust them.

For me, a leader is someone who cares about others, who is authentic in who they are, and who can show logic and guide people in the right direction. A leader is someone who helps other people rise up and find their own strengths.

TAMMEL

That trust triangle maps directly to what I see at the organizational level—when trust is the foundation, cultures transform. Andy Cunningham taught me early in my career, through something she called "The Cunningham Way" that culture is the brand. Absolutely everything flows from internal alignment. And what I find is that the leaders who build those cultures of trust are almost always deeply curious—about the people around them, and about what they don't yet know. Why is curiosity so essential?

LAI-DUMONE

Curiosity is essential to everyone. Curiosity leads to new possibilities, and I believe one of the roles of a leader is always leading people, leading teams and organizations to what's next, to what's new, through innovation and through change. The only way a leader can do that is to start getting curious— curious about the world around them, curious about their own ideas, and certainly curious about the ideas that the other people on their team have. Good leaders don't have all the answers, but they're curious to find the answers from the people on their team and from the world around them.

TAMMEL

And curiosity requires a certain kind of self-knowledge to work—because you can't be genuinely curious about others if you're still performing a version of yourself. The first thing I look at when I work with a leader isn't their strategy or their org chart. It's their ability to learn—even those they're leading—and practice self-awareness. From your perspective, what role does self-awareness play?

LAI-DUMONE

The most effective leaders are highly self-aware. They understand what their strengths are, what their weaknesses are, and they allow for that vulnerability to share both. In doing so, what they allow for is to give the best of themselves—and for other people to support them in the areas they need support in.

TAMMEL

And that's when everything else becomes possible. Not from a new strategy or restructuring—but a shift in how the leader listens. I call it building cultures of listening and learning. The moment true curiosity enters the room, ideas improve, trust becomes possible, and the culture starts to thrive. What does that look like for you?

LAI-DUMONE

I love this idea of listening and learning. When we are curious, particularly with other people, what we're doing is creating a space, a landscape, where possibility is available and trust is built. Being curious in the workplace means being curious about other people's ideas, making room for all ideas to make it to the table, and allowing people to share their ideas in an environment that's nonjudgmental. That right away builds trust.

When we are curious, we may have our own ideas, but we're open to other perspectives. When we allow that space for all ideas to come to the table, what we're doing is allowing the best ideas to make it to the finish line—and building psychological safety, because now people feel their ideas are welcomed.

TAMMEL

What separates the organizations that cultivate this—the curiosity, the creativity, the psychological safety—from the ones that quietly kill it?

LAI-DUMONE

From what I have seen, the organizations that invite in curiosity and creativity are what I call people-first organizations. They not only value profit, but they value people ahead of profit. They care about the people who work there. They want them to feel empowered, to work in an environment where they feel respected and where their ideas matter.

The companies that cultivate creativity understand that their most important asset is their people, and they are willing to invest in the ideas and the programming that allows their people to be developed and empowered.

TAMMEL

When you brought LEGO Serious Play into our CEO Collective circle, I watched something happen I have only seen a handful of times. Women leaders who had been holding back—accomplished, powerful women—suddenly started building with their hands, speaking from their models, leading with ideas they hadn't felt safe enough to say out loud. Something shifted in that room. Why does building something physical unlock what words alone cannot?

LAI-DUMONE

LEGO Serious Play is a facilitation methodology that started at the LEGO Group in the late nineties. The intention was to get people to think in different perspectives and use different tools as human beings to share ideas. As adults in the workplace, we're often in left-brain analytical thinking. But we have a whole other side of our brain—this creative side. It just makes practical sense that when you combine left-brain analytical thinking with right-brain creativity, especially tactile creativity, we come up with better ideas.

When we're sitting around asking people to share ideas, there may be people in the room who are never going to share even if an idea comes up in their head—because they're already judging their own idea. They might be thinking, who am I to share this? What if this idea is bad? Through LEGO Serious Play, everyone builds an idea, and then every single person has a chance to share. Everyone builds, everyone shares.

When you think about it as a tactile tool—you've built a model you can hold in your hand and point to as you speak. You're removing the idea from you and making it into something you can speak from. I refer to that as making the invisible visible, so you can share more readily.

And the rules of LEGO Serious Play—everyone builds, everyone shares, no judgment—build trust. After everyone builds their ideas, there is a process of collaboration, coming together and arriving at a singular idea to move forward with that incorporates a piece from everyone. So you are physically building better teams.

TAMMEL

That phrase *making the invisible visible* stays with me. Because vision works similarly. Until you can articulate it, it comes across more as a feeling than a direction.

How do you approach helping leaders take a vision that feels enormous and make it something they can move toward?

LAI-DUMONE

When I think about vision, I think about what I write about curiosity. Our visions come from what we are naturally curious about. And when you think about a vision—what you want to achieve—oftentimes it seems quite big, possibly unobtainable. The way I approach it is the idea of taking one small step at a time.

First, to have a vision, you have to have already paused and paid attention to what that curiosity is. So step one is already done. The second step is to ask what I call powerful questions—what if? How might I? How can it be done?—and really let yourself think in possibilities. Then the next part is to think about what's the smallest step you can take toward that vision. That's your creative action. It only has to be one small step.

Oftentimes we have this vision, this idea of the future, but if it's just a hope or a dream, we won't take action because it seems so broad and large and far away. But if we can break it down to one small step, then we can actually take creative action to start making it a possibility and a reality.

TAMMEL

Sometimes the pressure that forces those steps is enormous. You work with Navy SEALs and special forces operators through the Honor Foundation—people who have operated in genuinely life-or-death conditions. Having grown up with an uncle who was a Blue Angel and spent a lot of time learning from SEALs, I love to model leadership frameworks after them.

What have you taken from that work into what you now teach leaders in organizations?

LAI-DUMONE

I learned a lot by working with the special forces operators at the Honor Foundation. In the military, it's mission-oriented—it's literally, oftentimes, life or death. Looking at leading under pressure and resilient organizations, I see no better example than the military in terms of being able to have a mission, set a goal for success, and doing every single thing you need to reach that point. That may not mean your plan goes as planned, but it means being able to effectively pivot and change when necessary.

It's been a really great learning opportunity to understand the mindset and skill sets of resilience and pivoting and leading through change that these men and women have had to do throughout their careers.

TAMMEL

There's something I've always believed about titles—when they're right, they carry the whole philosophy in a handful of words. I love yours. Why a flying pig? What are you really asking us to consider?

LAI-DUMONE

The title comes from a long time ago when I was in college, back in 1993. I drove a little white Toyota Tercel—it was a little round car, looked like a little pig itself. I bought this polymer clay flying pig, about one inch big, and hung it from the rearview mirror with a fishing string. I had no air conditioning, so my windows were always down. And as I would drive up and down the Pacific Coast Highway, that little pig would just fly.

What I'm really asking us to consider is that anything we can put our minds to is possible—or at least, if you are thinking it, we can try to make it possible. With the steps of paying attention to that curiosity, asking questions like how might I, what if, what else can I do—and then just following through.

TAMMEL

You write that it's beyond our comfort zones that pigs can fly. I find that to be one of the most honest things anyone has written about growth—because the comfort zone is seductive. It feels like safety. What's the real relationship between discomfort and breakthrough?

LAI-DUMONE

The relationship between discomfort and breakthrough is the same for individuals and organizations. Discomfort is the gateway to breaking through legacy thinking—the way we've always done it—and to innovation. When we feel awkward, when we feel stretched, our brains are almost forced to find new pathways. It's in that tension where new skills and ideas and even new identities can emerge.

A lot of companies want to be innovative and have creative cultures, but the way they operate is through predictability and doing things the way they've always done it.

To create an area of change and a little bit of discomfort really allows people to thrive and tap into their curiosity and creativity.

We need to create an environment of psychological safety where leaders let people know it's okay to fail quickly, it's okay to try new things even if they don't work out. We want people experimenting.

TAMMEL

Growing up surrounded by the Vietnamese community, now living and working within the Vietnamese community in Orange County, I've witnessed something I don't think the business world has fully named.

After having worked with leaders who spanned six continents, the qualities I see in Vietnamese business leaders—perseverance across generations, building trust through relationships, instinctively lifting others as you climb, intelligence that reads what isn't being more clearly than what is, and taking the long view—these are some of the most powerful leadership qualities in the world.

With Vietnam taking the place it is on the global stage, how would you describe what the Vietnamese culture brings to global commerce?

LAI-DUMONE

It's so interesting for me to see this happening over the last several years. Being a Vietnamese refugee, coming over here fleeing the Communist Party, and seeing now that Vietnam is really adapting and being part of global commerce. The Vietnamese culture brings a sense of resilience, relational depth—because we had conflict as well as relationship with many different cultures and countries—and it's very adaptive.

The Vietnamese history has cultivated a sense of perseverance, always having to rise through challenges on an individual level and on a cultural level. That shows up in business as grit, as you can see from my mom's story on entrepreneurship. And because it is an Asian culture, the idea that trust is built through connection, through relationships, not just through agreements and contracts—in this global economy, being relational is a strategic advantage.

Vietnam is fairly new to this world of the global economy. For them to step out of where we came from—it's very youthful. I have some clients from Vietnam and they are so innovative, so creative, ambitious and playful. It's almost like a playground for them to join this global economy.

The balance between the heritage of the culture and being open to all this innovation—that combination of tradition and agility is really powerful.

TAMMEL

And then there are the qualities of Vietnamese women as leaders. What I see is something we rarely see in American leadership culture: ambition and genuine warmth. To be fierce and to be kind at the same time. To lead without abandoning what makes them worth following. How do you see Vietnamese women on the global stage?

LAI-DUMONE

Vietnamese women often lead from a place of relational intelligence. Historically balancing family, culture, and ambition, many develop resilience, emotional awareness, and collaborative influence. They don't separate authority from humanity.

In today's global environment, leadership must evolve. Command-and-control models are giving way to connection, inclusion, and adaptability. Leaders who can be decisive and compassionate, visionary and grounded, are better equipped for complexity.

What stands out about many Vietnamese women leaders is their ability to expand the definition of power. They don't abandon kindness to lead. They lead with it. They create belonging while driving progress.

And it may be one of the most sustainable models of leadership we have.

TAMMEL

Your practice of leaning into curiosity through worksmart Advantage, now brought to our circles that are changing the way women and men lead, is a true gift. When you get to where you're going with all of this—the book, the speaking, the work with leaders and teams—what does that look like? Who is Van Lai-DuMone at the destination?

LAI-DUMONE

Van Lai-DuMone at the destination is, in many ways, the same Van Lai she was at seven—curious, creative, and open to possibilities. The work I do today was never part of a carefully mapped plan. It grew because I followed my own framework: pause and pay attention to the curiosity tapping me on the shoulder, ask what if and how might I, and take one small step forward, even out of my comfort zone.

I see myself continuing to explore what's next, embracing new curiosities, and helping others unlock theirs. I also imagine a season where slowing down becomes part of the journey—making space to reflect, recharge, and notice the next opportunities.

The destination isn't a place. It's a mindset—following curiosity, creating impact, and living a life of possibility.

CULTURAL INTELLIGENCE AND THE NEW SPECIES
IN CONVERSATION WITH HÉLÈNE BLANCHETTE

Hélène Blanchette was presenting her Cultural Intelligence Center at World Trade Week — the annual gathering of international business leaders and global trade strategists in Orange County — when I realized she carries something rare: a genuine balance of global sensitivity, intellectual curiosity, and love for humanity.

The Cultural Intelligence Center is a platform Hélène is building at Chapman University's Schmid Center for International Business, where students and executives train with AI agents to prepare for cross-cultural business, then practice with live human mentors — closing the gap between how leaders think they come across and how they actually show up to interact in sensitive intercultural business settings. This is not simply a classroom exercise.

It represents the future of how we will prepare leaders to conduct business across borders.

Hélène spent over two decades as a senior executive at Xerox and Fuji Xerox, leading marketing across Canada before making history as the first woman Vice President of Fuji Xerox Asia Pacific — overseeing operations across fourteen countries from Singapore while navigating some of the most complex cultural and business terrain on earth. She later guided global marketing strategy from California. In January 2025, she spoke at Davos Lodge during the World Economic Forum on AI in higher education. Today, as Director of the Schmid Center for International Business at Chapman University, Hélène is building something I believe will reshape the way our next generation of leaders interacts.

When we sat down, Hélène brought global business wisdom at the highest level, cultural intelligence earned through decades of leading across languages and worldviews, and a visionary approach to artificial intelligence she designed to improve humanity—rather than displace it.

In my work with executives, conversations about AI are often framed as a binary: human or machine, efficiency or connection, progress or tradition. Hélène's Cultural Intelligence Platform imagines something new: a world where AI makes us better at being human, and where technology serves as the bridge to understanding rather than another wall between us.

At Chapman, Hélène is building a laboratory with four pillars — beginning with a Cultural Intelligence Center and a Global Applied Technology Center. This is not a theoretical exercise. It is a learning ecosystem designed to train students to manage AI agents as part of future-ready leadership, to develop AI-driven trade expertise, and to create intercultural learning grounded in human interaction and real-world negotiation. Her vision extends far beyond campus: Hélène imagines a Cultural Intelligence Platform accessible globally, where leaders prepare for international business by training with AI agents, then practice essential human phrases and interactions with live mentors to navigate cultural nuance with empathy and intelligence.

Similar to my work positioning global organizations through closing the gap between who they are and how the world perceives them, Hélène is working to close the gap between how leaders think they come across and how they actually are showing up for the cross-cultural relationships that determine everything. For any leader whose work crosses borders — and in today's economy, that is every leader worth their title — this conversation is essential.

ANNE TAMMEL

Hélène, to begin — what inspired you to step onto this leadership journey?

HÉLÈNE BLANCHETTE

For the past two decades, I've been an executive in Fujifilm — Fuji Xerox in Asia, and Xerox Corporation globally.

I spent ten years living in Singapore, responsible for fourteen countries. I was the first woman to become Vice President of Fuji Xerox Asia Pacific. It was fascinating — people often assume it must have been hard. Well, everything is hard, but it was more enriching and interesting. You get to know yourself so well through that.

Before that, I was in Canada, where I'm originally from. I was director of marketing across Canada for Xerox. Eight years ago, I moved to California for my husband — a big decision for me, leaving behind my career. He had already sacrificed a few years in Asia, and wanted to live here, closer to his daughter. It was tough, as a leader, being stripped from everything, starting new in a country without being able to work initially — I didn't have the working permit. The minute I got my green card, Xerox rehired me as Vice President of Marketing for Xerox Production globally. So, back to traveling again. Looking at my life, I've traveled across the world most of my life.

When I was younger, I started so young in business. At twenty-three, I was managing five tennis, squash, and racquetball clubs, with three restaurants, 25,000 members, and 350 employees. The owners lived in Florida, and I was in Montreal — they would show up twice a year. You learn to be responsible and to try everything. Innovation drove me from the start because I would try everything in marketing. I had no limits. I learned a lot through that.

TAMMEL

What strikes me in this story is your resilience — you stepped away from everything, moved to a new country without a work permit, and the moment you could, you were back leading at the global level. That says something about who you are as a leader. What would you consider the most important traits of an international leader?

BLANCHETTE

My personal values, first of all — integrity, honesty, and cultural respect. That's essential for an international leader. If you don't understand the value of different cultures, you miss so much.

Being visionary, a gatherer of people, making people embrace your vision and wanting to make it happen — that's important. Accepting and letting people bring their own sauce — you don't possess the truth; you're just bringing the right people together to make it happen. You must have your ego in check.

Visionary people sometimes become toxic because of ego, or become hyper-controlling micromanagers. Both scenarios turn sour. Balance is one of the most important things in leadership.

TAMMEL

That philosophy — gathering people, letting them bring their own identity and perspective, keeping ego in check — you're translating that into something concrete at Chapman. Can you tell us about the lab you're building?

BLANCHETTE

My vision, when starting somewhere, is always the same approach: what's going on now, why is it happening, what needs to be done, and what can the organization absorb? Where does it fit in?

The first thing I did at Chapman was look at global trends — AI, sustainability solutions, digital transformation, globalized trade. These trends are undeniable. Then, how do we educate students to be future-ready — not necessarily for what we've been doing the last four decades? That's how we created the Schmid Center for International Business, which existed as a name and entity, but not as a structure. Now, I've built four pillars for this structure. The first pillar is a Cultural Intelligence Center; another is a Global Applied Technology Center. We're not creating new technology but applying existing technology to provide business solutions.

One of our initial projects within this applied center is developing an AI-driven trade expert agent. This agent helps businesses in languages they're comfortable with, to interact and understand international trade dynamics as they evolve. These first two pillars — the Cultural Intelligence Center and Applied Technology — will be built by students, under our guidance, creating a learning and contributing platform.

We'll also teach them important skills for the future: managing an AI workforce. They'll live in a world with AI companions. Companies today might have thirty to fifty employees, but only six or seven humans — the rest are AI. These AI agents must be managed differently from humans. It takes several hours daily. We're teaching students how to become leaders who manage and control AI agents effectively.

Additionally, we're developing a shadowing program, exposing students to international leaders, and providing seats for underrepresented communities. We have brilliant people who could benefit from the Cultural Intelligence Center — for interviews, understanding integration into a new environment, whether it's immigrants or international companies entering the U.S. market.

Our goal is to become a hub of multicultural intelligence, trade, and innovation. And we won't stop at trade. After the trade agent is built and maintained, we'll move on to other solutions — maybe sustainable solutions with international impact.

All this connects to our third pillar: creating high-paying jobs and internships. We want as many companies from the real business world participating, offering interaction, providing solutions, creating learning platforms, and helping our students secure internships and great jobs.

TAMMEL

What you're building addresses something real. Anyone who has gone into another country and tried doing business without truly understanding that culture — because you cannot learn that from a textbook — has run into barriers that can immediately ruin a business deal.

BLANCHETTE

Especially coming from the United States, which is so transactional, versus Asia, which is so relational. We don't think of business the same way. Here, we think, one transaction, big deal, fantastic.

There, they're looking at you as, will you be a lifetime partner? So let's get to know each other. A very different approach. I want to have a human component, too. It's one thing to learn how to bow. It's another to do it in front of a human. One of the learning curves would be to have that human interaction after you've learned how to do business with someone.

TAMMEL

We're highly individualistic in America. Since most countries aren't, how does your center address that gap?

BLANCHETTE

It's a matter of exposure and understanding. First, anyone coming into the Cultural Intelligence Center would identify who they are through a questionnaire and interaction: their values, how they see life, which lens they look through, their family nucleus, their basic values. All of that composes who you are, how you think, how you judge. This is crucial. I do this currently with my international marketing students, and they find it fascinating afterward to share what's common and uncommon among them.

If you focus afterward on what you have in common, you'll have a great first interaction. If you're aware of what's uncommon in your culture versus theirs, you have a learning curve, and you'll become more intelligent towards that.

That's why I call it the Cultural Intelligence Center — it's about being intelligent and respectful towards someone else's culture. That's the most important part of doing business internationally.

TAMMEL

The best leaders I know are lifelong learners. I don't believe you can lead unless you're in a constant state of learning. You mentioned you're not from academia — what has that experience been like? You described it as building a spaceship?

BLANCHETTE

Yes, it's been quite a ride. In January, I was in Davos for the World Economic Forum. I came back, and five days later, I started teaching two classes. I'd never taught before. I didn't know how to do a syllabus or anything. Every day, literally, I was building the plane midair. It was a significant challenge. For the last five months, it's been a massive endeavor — building my courses daily, teaching them at night, and simultaneously learning what the students expected. How detailed do they want things? I didn't realize how detailed academia required me to be, because I've always interacted with leaders and directors, or my employees, and you don't have to go into all the details. You can just say, "Go research this and come back." You don't need to tell them, "I'm going to judge you five points on this." You don't provide that kind of structure normally. So it was quite confusing for me, and I'm sure confusing for the students as well. However, I compensated with innovation and passion. And obviously, teaching international marketing wasn't a foreign field for me — I brought a lot of real-life experience into it — but it was still quite a challenge. Today with the combination of experience and academia, it is a smooth ride.

TAMMEL

That's the tension so many leaders face when they move between worlds — the corporate instinct says move fast, trust your people, skip the details. Academia wants structure. How do you integrate those two mindsets to create something people can actually use?

BLANCHETTE

It's especially challenging when you have a change of Dean in between, because you have to start over explaining your vision and views. But I think overall, if it makes sense, people will understand, even if they might not grasp all the details initially. I remember when I did the digital transformation at Fuji Xerox in Asia, a Japanese company traditionally reluctant to change, I realized when people don't make decisions or push away ideas, it's because they don't understand what you're talking about. They won't say "I don't understand." Instead, they'll say, "I need to think about that," because they need time to comprehend what you're presenting.

People don't want to appear uninformed — their ego takes a stand: "How come I don't know that?" With something like AI disrupting the world, the key is making it understandable through concrete storytelling: "Imagine this," "Imagine that." For example, if you want to talk about AI management, remind them of when social media was created. The most important job on the market was "Social Media Manager." Fifteen or eighteen years ago, a Social Media Manager was one of the highest-paid jobs, starting at $150,000, and people asked, "Is that even a real job? They just spend all day on Facebook." But it was a real job and was in high demand. Today, AI managers are going to be a highly demanded job too. So if you explain AI management through the lens of social media, people can understand what you're talking about in your spaceship.

TAMMEL

The spaceship you're building while flying?

BLANCHETTE

Exactly. Because AI is a new species. It's not just technology, not just a new thing — it's a completely new species. We have to learn how to cope, live with it, and manage it.

TAMMEL

That reframe is important — a new species, not just a new tool. You've built the Cultural Intelligence Center for students. Do you have a vision for bringing this model into the world of international business, for leaders who need it?

BLANCHETTE

That's the beauty of digital. Online AI agents mean this platform will eventually be open globally. Initially, you need a period to build, deploy, and learn in a controlled environment. But once we have that, we plan to make the Cultural Intelligence Platform accessible from home.

People will be able to prepare a deal or a meeting with a Chinese counterpart or any international business scenario. Currently, people rely on their personal connections for immediate cultural information. Instead, you'll be interacting with someone who might look like me but is actually an AI agent — or literally a Chinese person if that's the interaction you want — speaking your language fluently because it's an AI, and practicing your own deal with this agent.

TAMMEL

Earlier you said it's one thing to learn how to bow, but another to do it in front of a human. So the agent gives you the preparation, but the real test is still human.

BLANCHETTE

Yes. Online training, of course, but also — especially for students or people physically coming to Chapman university — I want a component of human interaction. After the online interaction, they'd have real preparation, practice saying how you give and take something. For example, in Asia you should hand business cards a certain way. How do you take it? What do you do once it's in your hand? What are all the faux pas you could commit?

I see many faux pas from Americans. They'll take the card — "Oh, thank you" — put it immediately in their pocket without looking, or write notes right on the business card.

That's a huge insult. For an Asian person, a business card represents years of hard work reaching their position. You should pause, look at it, read it, and show respect for that accomplishment. Writing on it disrespects something very important.

TAMMEL

Those small nuances are sometimes everything. They could make or break decades of business over something as simple as a business card.

BLANCHETTE

Saying sorry in Asia is a sign of intelligence. In America, it can be perceived as weakness. But in Asia, it means: "I avoided conflict. I didn't make you lose face; I didn't lose face." These small examples amplify when you're making important business deals.

TAMMEL

How long can someone expect to spend in the Cultural Intelligence Center if they're preparing to do business in a country they've never visited?

BLANCHETTE

Probably a couple of hours, depending on the depth needed. If you're an expatriate or planning extensive time, it's a different preparation than just a short visit. I'd say about forty-five minutes to an hour just to understand and accept who you are — that's step one. Then, from there, start training. Altogether, about three to five hours would be a good foundational training. You can't cover everything, but that's a solid base. Eventually, people will access it from home. The first year, students will build it, with experts contributing content and accuracy. The agent's interactions will be carefully managed for at least the first year and daily thereafter to ensure accuracy, ensuring the Thai agent doesn't start turning Chinese.

TAMMEL

Because agents keep learning — they don't sleep.

BLANCHETTE

Agents keep learning, evolving constantly. They can start hallucinating by gaining content and drawing their own conclusions, sometimes creatively going off-course. They must be carefully managed daily.

TAMMEL

That raises the real question for leaders.

If I'm training with an agent I believe is preparing me for a deal in China, and the agent is hallucinating, how do you manage that?

BLANCHETTE

The beauty of what we're trying to teach is that it's not just a one-time "build it and it runs on its own" scenario.

Think about an adolescent. You've given them lessons, you've given them knowledge, and then they go into the real world. You still keep them in check on a daily basis, right?

I'm trying to make it simple, but at the end of the day, it requires that you verify and monitor what the agents create. You have questions to ask, or ways to read what the agent has created. And then obviously, feedback would come in from people who interact with it, saying, "Oh, it said that? That's weird." Then you're able to check, "Why did it go there? Why did it say that?"

I don't think it's necessarily going to affect a business deal negatively, but it could, for instance, take a cultural aspect from another country — such as "Don't touch the head of children," because it's an insult, which applies in Thailand but not necessarily in Singapore — and mistakenly apply it elsewhere. That could be a hallucination the agent creates by coming to its own conclusion. But that's exactly what managing AI agents is all about — controlling your toddler.

TAMMEL

A very intelligent toddler.

BLANCHETTE

Yes, but that's the new kind of responsibility leaders will need to learn. My collaborator Luis Salazar, CEO of AI4SP — who is a specialist in AI — agrees.

He's very experienced in managing agents; he has his own company with about fifty agents, so he understands how to manage that well.

TAMMEL

What I find extraordinary about your vision is that you're using AI to bring us closer together as humans. That's not the conversation most people are having. How will people connect, do business, and collaborate better as humans as a result of what you're building?

BLANCHETTE

I've always said it's all about knowledge. When I lived in Singapore — Singapore is mostly Buddhist, surrounded by 250 million Muslims — I never had a problem. Fabulous people I met throughout that experience. It's not true that Islam is terrible, but that's the only part we often convey. Yet actually, 99.9% of the people are extremely peaceful, nice people who care about their children, who care about the same things you do. Yet we villainize people because we're not knowledgeable enough about who they are, their daily life, or how they think. If we judged all Americans from certain individuals, we'd form a false impression. It's true for every culture, every way.

And I meant it when I said we would not need as many weapons. I was speechless when, at the forum, the person before me spoke about artificial intelligence weapons. The whole crowd went silent — you felt you were entering a world of evil. It felt like doomsday. It was so scary. But I sincerely believe that with greater cultural intelligence, we wouldn't need that as much.

TAMMEL

I have profound respect for what you're doing. You're taking AI — when usually the conversation revolves around replacing human connection — and tapping into this new species in a way that might make us better humans.

BLANCHETTE

Better communicators. Because it's all about communication.

TAMMEL

What advice would you give to young people entering this landscape? At World Trade Week, you juxtaposed two visions: one terrifying view of AI and then yours, which was a genuine breakthrough. What do the next generation of leaders need to understand?

BLANCHETTE

We're not just inventing a technology; we've created a new species. We absolutely cannot use that species to become dumber. I see a lot of students who — if I ask a question, they'll just plug it into AI, and I'll get thirty identical essays. That makes no sense to me — grading essays made by AI. What I want them to understand is this species will bring great efficiency, absolutely, but it's not mature enough yet to discern good from bad. I have fifty years of experience that I built on building blocks through reading, learning, and experiencing. When you're twenty years old, you don't have that. When I interact with AI, I say, "Bring efficiency. I'll take that, I'll judge the veracity of that — no, that's not a good reference or a valid point," because I have critical thinking based on my experience. At twenty, they find AI awesome because it does their work, they don't have to work as hard. But that cheats their brain. This can rot their brain and I don't want them to become dumber. That's the danger I don't want them to face.

I want them to use AI for efficiency, but I want them to develop critical thinking. The methodology we're proposing — creating solutions, understanding company challenges, solving problems, learning how to become AI managers — gives them the full cycle of critical thinking they'll need. If I can play a part in helping youth move forward into that future, I'll be very happy. Let's see if we find the funding and make it happen.

TAMMEL

We discussed the traits of great leadership earlier. Is there anything you'd add specifically about leading an AI system?

BLANCHETTE

Critical thinking is key. It's especially important to develop as a young person. If you want to be a leader, you must have experience with critical thinking. I'm also on the board of the Child Creativity Lab, helping develop critical thinking in youth by using everyday objects, items from recycling bins, and then making them create projects without instructions. We give them challenges like building a zipline from toilet paper rolls, buttons, and household items. They must create and think critically toward an end goal.

These methods are important for educating future leaders, helping them understand what's right, what's wrong, why we do things — is it the best way? How do I properly manage my company so that I have a good balance between the human workforce and the AI workforce of the future?

SACRED SPACE, TRANSFORMED LIVES

IN CONVERSATION WITH BONNI POMUSH

Bonni Pomush, CEO of Working Wardrobes, stands as one of the most remarkable leaders I have encountered in Orange County — and I have sat across from many. In the decades I have spent working with executives, I've learned that leaders who transform organizations share a particular quality: an unwavering belief that every person in the room carries unrealized potential, and that it is the leader's sacred responsibility to help them find it. Bonni has this. She has it in abundance.

As Bonni explains, "Just like flowers know to grow into flowers... we were built to be something... what an honor it is to discover that and give it." She lives that. Every person who walks through her doors feels the genuine love she radiates.

When I walked through the doors of Working Wardrobes and she took me on a tour, I understood why. Working

Wardrobes is designed with the same intentionality a great architect brings to space. The pod Bonni showed me — a glass-walled room within an open office, simultaneously private and connected — told me everything I needed to know about how she thinks. Sacred space is not a metaphor here. It is architecture.

I was proud to join Bonni on the Working Wardrobes podcast *Real Talk. Real Growth.* and share a two-way conversation on leadership, culture, building sacred spaces, and what happens when women come together to honor a vision and co-create something greater than themselves.

There is great purpose and power behind everything Bonni does, and her landmark event, Working Wardrobes' inaugural Power Within Luncheon at the Balboa Bay Club — the first of its kind in Orange County — promises to be as transformative as her organization.

Bonni has led Working Wardrobes through a transformation that organizational theorists study and practitioners rarely achieve: a Glassdoor rating moved from 2.3 to 4.3 in two years. The number of clients served tripled. The culture shifted from institution to ecosystem. These are not accidental results. They are the product of a leader who decided, early, that her tombstone would not read "answered every email."

Working Wardrobes serves people who have lived in their cars, women emerging from the most devastating domestic violence situations, veterans, the formerly incarcerated — people the world has told, in a hundred different ways, that the door is closed. Bonni opens the door. She does not simply offer them a wardrobe. She offers them a new operating system. Soft skills. Self-awareness. The belief that they can become someone the world has not yet seen.

When I asked what Bonni brings from her background in government and education to this role, she told me about being an introverted child who learned acutely what it feels like not to be included — and made a decision that no room she led would ever make someone feel that way. That is the origin story of a leader.

I left Working Wardrobes knowing two things: that Bonni Pomush is one of the most effective leaders in Orange County today, and that what she has built here is a model — not just for nonprofits, but for every organization that wants to understand what it looks like when a leader puts people first without apology.

ANNE TAMMEL

Bonni, what you've built here — in the middle of a place where so many difficult things happen — is a space where people arrive in crisis and leave as leaders. You've transformed something almost improbable into reality, which fascinates me. Because in my world — coming from Silicon Valley and tech — leadership is measured by outcomes. All that matters is your success story. If you don't have one, you're very quickly out. But you clearly have remarkable success story after success story — backed up by data. We know it's real.

So can we start at the beginning? Can you walk us through your leadership journey? Where did this start, and what drew you to this work?

BONNI POMUSH

I think I can best start my leadership story with a story that my mom tells. I was about two years old, playing with my little kitchenette set. I had a chair on top of a table, and I was sitting on the chair doing something. My mom came over and said, *Bonni, what are you playing?* And I said, *bossing.* She said, *Whho are you bossing?* And I said, *everyone.*

I think I was built for leadership — whether I wanted it or not. It's part of my DNA and who I am. For all of the times I can remember, from childhood through young adulthood through adulthood, I've been in positions, whether formal or informal, where people looked to me to help guide the way. How we're going to solve the problem together. How we're going to really capture the future, harness the opportunity, create a vision and pursue it.

What's drawn me to this space is really my true north as a human. What's my why? Why am I here? In one part, it's to maximize the talents and skills I have and show up in the world the best I can — and to help other people do the same. Every position I've ever had has allowed me to do that on scale.

I love this tagline at Working Wardrobes: *Your future, our purpose.* We are laser focused on helping you create your future.

That is our purpose — to help people tap into their potential and live it well.

TAMMEL

You're here as the leader who sets the tone for every interaction, every impression — new hires, clients, the community. I talk about this often, and some leaders treat the topic like it's foreign. But especially for nonprofits — here we are, having just toured a space where people who arrived living in their cars are now leading. In technology we call it the end user. How do you see the ripple of what you're creating?

POMUSH

I think it's the magic of being alive and the universe. It's this X Factor — you don't really ever know what you're exactly setting into motion. You know maybe part one, part two, part three, but you have no sense of the infinite ripple effects. When I think about Working Wardrobes clients, I think about generations. Sure, we're absolutely helping one person in this moment — but play that out. We've reached over 142,000 people on these journeys. Multiply that to their family, their home, their neighborhood, their community. And it goes and goes and goes. I don't think it ever ends.

TAMMEL

Leadership has changed so dramatically — especially for women. I've watched it shift from one woman who had to claw her way to the top and keep people down just to hold her position, to something entirely different. Can you speak to leadership today in relation to where it was when you began your career?

POMUSH

I've definitely experienced this paradigm shift — from authoritarian, do it because I said so, I am the leader, that is all — to facilitative, adaptive, collaborative leadership. The leadership I espouse is not hierarchical at all. It is always a flat organization with different talents and unique contributions made by different players on the team, and it's the role of the leader to make sure we maximize those opportunities.

Just like with our clients, every person has unique potential, unique purpose, and I believe it's a sacred thing to help them unlock it and share it in the world. When I think about leadership today, I think about it less in a hierarchical way and more in a collaborative, relational way — not transactions. The long game. I'm investing in you. I want you to grow personally and professionally while you're here. How do I let you know it's safe to be fully you here, and then invite that part of you that is unique and able to contribute, on full display.

TAMMEL

Clearly it's worked. Your Glassdoor rating went from 2.3 to 4.3 in two years. You tripled the number of clients you serve. How did you build that?

POMUSH

The first three years of my leadership at Working Wardrobes were really about modernizing the organization. I use this analogy: if you've ever remodeled a house, it's the unsexy stuff no one sees — the plumbing, the infrastructure, the windows.

We replaced a lot of things you don't see, but that give us the opportunity to optimize our reach and make more impact.

Now that we've modernized our systems, we're in the process of optimizing.

And no matter what we're doing, it's with people, by people, for people. People are always our first priority. Some of our new hires — particularly on the management and leadership team — have shared with me that, in contrast to other places they've worked, they're taken aback by our focus on people.

How we lead our people, how we mentor our people, how we resource our people. That's a key component of this success.

TAMMEL

You showed me the glass-walled room within the open office. You're intentionally creating sacred spaces where people can develop trust. Can you share more about how you think about physical space as a leadership tool?

POMUSH

Optum sponsors our pod, and they share this value — that privacy matters, that a sacred space is something you create both physically and emotionally, and both of those components have to be present.

We're in an open office setting, so whoever is talking, everybody can hear. If someone is pouring their soul out to a counselor, they may not want an audience for that.

The pod creates a private space — but it has glass windows on both sides, so while you're in the cocoon of a safe, confidential space, you're still not locked out from the rest of what's going on.

You can see what's happening in front of and behind you. That creates psychological safety.

Many of our clients are facing post-traumatic stress and different trauma responses — normative responses to what they've been through.

It's incumbent on us to honor that and give it its own space.

TAMMEL

And how do you create that metaphorical pod for each employee who walks in every day?

POMUSH

This is actually a shared responsibility, and the way we share it is that we hire for our core values.

Humble achiever — we leave our ego at the door. We know that no one can do anything unless we're all doing what we each do differently.

Thoughtful relator — no two people are the same, so don't treat two people the same. I need to meet you where you are.

Grit — not hold-on-for-dear-life grit, but embrace-the-adventure grit. We don't always know how we're going to get there, but we see the vision clearly, and we'll go for the adventure of getting there.

And our final value is integrity. Not just doing the right thing when no one's looking — we're talking about building systems to last. Teach them how to fish. That Maimonides principle: feed a person for a day, or teach them to feed themselves for a lifetime. That is integrity.

We're helping people update their operating systems with soft skills that will serve them for a lifetime of career success.

TAMMEL

You work with veterans, with those who've been incarcerated, with women who are walking away from the most devastating situations—often with nothing. And you see the possibility in every one of them. Can you share more about what some of these clients bring to organizations, having gone through surviving the worst aspects of life then thriving through this transformative process, that maybe others don't?

POMUSH

They have done a lot of reps in the gym on resilience. They have very strong muscles of get back up and go again. And that inspires the heck out of me.

I don't pretend to say I've lived through a lot of hardships. So when I think about where they have been, how they have overcome, and how much it took to even walk in the door here — I think it's so difficult to ask for help.

And here is a person putting their humility at the front and saying, I need help. I want to get here. Can you please help me get there?

To be met there — with acceptance, not being judged by where you've been or your mistakes or what's happened to you, but focused entirely on where you're headed — that's everything. That's seeing and living in possibility.

TAMMEL

Emily Dickinson said, *I dwell in possibility.* You're clearly giving that ability to dwell in possibility. And when you dwell in possibility, everything becomes possible.

Can we talk about leadership traits? What are some of the leadership qualities — the ones we were once told that's a woman trait that doesn't belong in a boardroom — that have gotten you and this organization to where you are today?

POMUSH

I've always been an achiever, and I really tied my worthiness to what I achieved and what I produced and what I got done. And I got sick from doing that — literally.

What I learned from going through that experience was that at the end of the day — my tombstone is not going to read, I did these 52 projects really great. My headstone is not going to say I answered every email. At the end, it's going to matter how I treated people and how I showed up and how I connected with my fellow humans.

When I heard for the first time the Maya Angelou insight — that people don't remember what you said, they don't remember what you did, but they always remember how you made them feel — I got it. I saw my true north in that moment. Ever since, this is how I evaluate myself at the end of the day. Not did I answer those emails — of course

I'm running through that all day. But what matters when I lay my head down at night is: how did I treat people? How did I show up with humans? That's been my leadership strategy, through and through.

TAMMEL

Working Wardrobes is hosting the Power Within Luncheon — which SoCal Women in Business and OC CEO Collective are so proud to partner on. What's the essence of this event?

POMUSH

I am so excited about this event. If you are a fabulous, fierce female, this is for you. It will be a very chic luncheon with a fashion show and shopping. But the part I cannot wait for is to hear from our five community-nominated panelists — we're going to hear their stories, their journeys of overcoming, these unique ways they have really showcased their power within themselves to become who they are.

Please visit workingwardrobes.org for tickets and details. I also want to highlight that our founder Jerri Rosen wrote a memoir about how she built Working Wardrobes — available as a bundle with Power Within tickets. It captures the most beautiful pictures and stories about how Working Wardrobes became the gem of Orange County that it is.

TAMMEL

For those who want to get involved at a deeper level — how do they connect with you?

POMUSH

Reach out, connect with us. Email developmentteam@workingwardrobes.org and we can learn what it is you're after and help connect you to create that experience. We're very creative here, and we are all thoughtful relators — we really meet people where they are. Let us know what you're interested in — we'll figure out a way to make it happen.

TAMMEL

You've been named Woman of the Year by OC Women to Women and one of the OC Register's most influential leaders. What is the state of women's leadership in Orange County today — and where are we going?

POMUSH

I think we're still catching up, and it pains me to say that. We're still making 80 to 84 cents on the dollar that men make, and that to me is unacceptable. But I am seeing more and more women leaders coming up the ranks, and what I'm physically noticing is how much we collaborate, connect, and work together. This marketplace needs more collaboration — maximizing the strengths we already have.

And I think allyship is another big shift. My experience, particularly here in Orange County with the women leaders I know, is much more rooted in allyship — how can I sponsor you, help you, support you on your journey? We have a group we call the Sisters in Good — CEOs of nonprofits here in Orange County who embody this. Collaborators, allies, wanting to see the best for everyone.

TAMMEL

That circle of collaboration — that's where the future is being built. When women unite and celebrate what's strong and unique about each other, imagine what we will achieve. When you fully actualize your vision for Working Wardrobes — what does that look like?

POMUSH

I've got dreams. We really want to make sure we have an accessible presence throughout Orange County, and we believe the best way to do that is through mobile service units — vehicles out on the road that can provide our soft skill training and our signature wardrobe service where our clients are.

We also turned 35 last year as an organization, and we want to own our own home. If any of your listeners have a warehouse around 10,000 square feet to offer at low rent or even free for a period of time, we will be very interested. We need semi-truck access, plenty of parking and restrooms, on that 55 corridor.

And we know that our clients need help with AI essentials and entrepreneurship essentials in this marketplace. We're working with five generations in the workforce right now — that's a lot of flexing your style to different personalities. Through it all, we envision Working Wardrobes continuing to be this award-winning, highly respected service provider and workplace, building systems to last, treating people with integrity.

TAMMEL

Your background — government leadership, education, the entrepreneurial spirit you've built across sectors — can you take us through the journey that brought you here?

POMUSH

Early in my career, I loved being a supplementary school teacher and an overnight camp counselor, and that parlayed into leadership positions running the camps and after-school programs. As a child, I was very introverted and became sensitive, as an adult, to some of the things that made me feel uncomfortable as a child — not being included, not being welcomed, not being integrated into the whole. That really changed the way I show up. I want to bring people in. I want to ensure people are seen and heard and acknowledged.

I then went into the government side of my career, working for the city and a school district. Those roles really developed my entrepreneurial spirit — leading programs that raised money to support in-classroom funding, learning the marketplace of demand and supply. Whether it was childcare or athletics or yoga or enrichment classes, we could maximize government-funded resources to catalyze community.

Moving to California and entering the nonprofit sector gave me such pride in learning how collaborative Orange County is — what a unique place on the map. The nonprofit sector is so integrated into the business sector, and the business players in our community understand very much that they need high-quality employees for their business, a framework of people to connect their brand to. There are all these mutually beneficial things that happen when nonprofits and for-profits get together.

Coming to Working Wardrobes has really brought all of those pieces together — from how we treat an individual to how we create programs that meet communal needs while operating on the individual layer. And no matter what we're doing, it's from a place of pure dignity. I quote often Heidi Zuckerman with this one — she talked about a basic human need that we all share: to be seen, to be heard, to be loved. And I want to be a part of meeting that need for people.

TAMMEL

When you get to where you're going as a leader — what's happening, who are you, what have you built along the way?

POMUSH

My greatest hope is that I become my best self — and that I help other people become their best selves. I have developed many leaders over my career, and I want to grow more. More people who are self-actualized and able to be their best version of themselves, which also means helping more people do the same.

I think each of us is here for a different purpose. I firmly believe we each have unique gifts to give. And that is a calling — an invitation built into us. To help myself and other people live their purpose. Live with purpose, for purpose, on purpose. That's what I'm looking for.

TAMMEL

I believe that once you discover your true purpose, nothing can stop you from achieving it. Whatever hardships you face along the way— those are there to make you stronger and more resilient. But it's always there. It's waiting.

What does it look like to you when we're all achieving our own unique purpose?

POMUSH

It's like a fabric that doesn't exist yet — all these interwoven threads that create something so much bigger than what we can even see.

On a very spiritual level — flowers know to grow into flowers. They reach, somehow, for the sun. They figure out how to reach for the water. And they become a flower. Humans are built with the same characteristics — we were built to be something and that is our unique offering in the world. What an honor it is to discover that and give it.

WOMEN RISING IN LEADERSHIP
IN CONVERSATION WITH LACY SCHOEN

L acy Schoen is the President and CEO of the Brea Chamber of Commerce and is the Founder of the Women Rising Leadership Academy, a research-backed leadership program now expanding from California to audiences across the United States and internationally. She has been devoted to seeing the face of leadership in organizations change to represent more female leaders for the last 12 years. Not only has she created Women Rising Leadership Academy—a California based program now being introduced to the entire nation—she is also working to educate male executive leaders about the profitability associated with women in top leadership roles. Through this education, Lacy offers a leadership blueprint—backed by research—that guides leaders through proven ways to lead better organizations that include gender balance and in the process, makes them more profitable.

Having spent decades advising and coaching women in the workforce—including many rising through the ranks—I was more than familiar with the challenges women face in leadership. But it was when I met Lacy and became involved with her organization that I started to understand the unique challenges faced by women in middle management. Since it has always been my style to start at the top and create my own, it has been a powerful and meaningful process to learn from Lacy—and from the uniquely driven women I have worked with and gotten to know through the Women Rising Leadership Academy.

ANNE TAMMEL

Lacy, can we hear about your journey—what brought you into all of this and what you're doing with the Women Rising Leadership Academy?

LACY SCHOEN

Thanks for having me, Anne. I've been 40 years in nonprofit management, and I decided to retire in 2016. I had become a certified coach because I was really interested in helping women succeed, and I became really interested in why there aren't more women in the top levels of leadership in corporate America.

There's no shortage of research on that. If we want to know, it's discoverable why we're not there. One of the reasons I wanted to coach is I felt I hadn't received a lot of support from women from my generation, and I just wanted to change that and be a force for good. But I also wanted to do something very practical. I didn't want to scream and shout about what should be. I wanted to deal with what is, the current state of things. The research is so valuable because if we know the causes of why there's not more women at the top, then most likely we're going to be able to deal with those reasons. So I was able to categorize the barriers of women getting to the top into two categories: internal barriers and external barriers.

I was invited at Cal State Fullerton to become part of the Board for their women's leadership program. I let them know if we're not doing something novel or unique, it's going to be really hard to grow the program and to fundraise for it. But if we really want to wrap our curriculum around overcoming barriers, I think I can bring a lot of money to the table. So they allowed me to do that, and their board voted to change the curriculum to overcoming barriers in every workshop based on research and science. That was 10 years ago, and it's a proven curriculum. We found that female students were graduating and getting promoted more quickly than their peers at great organizations like Deloitte and OptumRx and Google.

I really became passionate about delivering the program to working women. I saw this Brea Chamber of Commerce job looking for a CEO. I thought, this is a really good marriage. If the board is interested in this program, then I would be interested in this job. So we absolutely aligned. That was in

2022 and we launched the program, and it's just grown tremendously ever since.

TAMMEL

Four years you launched it. I'm amazed at how much progress that quickly. And what's unique about the curriculum that makes it so effective?

SCHOEN

A couple of things. One, I think it's based on research and science. One of the workshops is male female work culture differences, because males and females do have different culture, and it starts from birth. There's science behind how we're different, our chemical makeup, our biological makeup, our physiological makeup, it's all different along with the way we're socialized. Wrapping something around that is unusual for a women's leadership curriculum. That workshop is one of the favorites of most women. It's the most eye opening because most men and most women understand that at times we don't understand each other, but they really don't understand we are completely living in different worlds, and to understand the other's world is to be able to start to live and be powerful in it.

I think truth telling is very unique. We create a safe space where the women can talk about the struggles they're having, the bias that they face, and they find out that they're not alone. When I ask speakers to be part of this, my agreement with them is that they truth tell and that they talk about the real challenges, the real bias, the real struggles that they face, so that the women in the program can see that a woman in a top leadership position has overcome the things that she herself is dealing with.

TAMMEL

You were talking about this program to educate executives internally at organizations about the value of women in leadership and what we bring to organizations, even from a profitability standpoint.

SCHOEN

Absolutely 100%. It's also one of those things that's been studied well, and that is that you do think differently, and that does increase profits. There are several entrepreneurial leaders in the world who are discovering this through their own experiences. One of them that I love to talk about is Kevin O'Leary, who's a shark on Shark Tank, and he talks about how he is now to the point where he seeks out women-run businesses, because 75% of his profits in his portfolio are coming from women-run businesses. And he started talking about this about six years ago, and he said, "I'm going to look at why this is. What are the women doing differently?"

And he found they were doing three things differently. One, they set more realistic goals. So the men would have these very lofty goals and meet them like 40% of the time, and the women would have less lofty goals, but they would meet them 95% of the time, and then that resulted in more stable companies, so they had less turnover.

He also says that the women were more collaborative, and he talks about how they also prioritize well. And he says that of all of his women-run companies in his portfolio, I think all of them but one are mothers. And he says that mothers are put in these impossible circumstances all the time and can only do the most important things, and that translates to business.

So he said, "My women business leaders, they don't waste their time on unnecessary things. They don't spin their wheels because they know they can't get everything done. So they only do the most important things," and the men, not so much.

So what he did is, he got all his companies together and said to the guys, "This is how the women are doing it. And if you do the same things, we'll all make more money." So it was teaching the men to operate more like the women.

And he said they did it, and a year later, they had a 15% increase in the portfolio. It was 15 billion, it went to 17.5, so two and a half billion dollars more in that portfolio, just by doing things the way the women were doing them.

I think that's a pretty strong statement for the profitability of the female approach to business.

TAMMEL

And this is men just modeling an approach created by women? Can you share any success stories coming out of the program?

SCHOEN

I think what is staggering to me is how universal some of these experiences are. One of the ones I hear the most is "I thought I needed to be a cookie cutter of the leadership I saw above me. And it's been thrilling to not only understand that I can be a good leader without leading like they do, but that is absolutely imperative to my success, that I find my own leadership style." That is exactly the realization: I was trying to be like everybody else, not realizing that wasn't the path to success.

A lot of women don't realize that men negotiate their salary, and most women don't. Most women do believe that they will be paid fairly only to find out that they're not. Our most recent impact survey showed that nearly 40% of the women who graduated were able to negotiate some type of compensation increase. So that says that people are not necessarily holding women back. In some cases, we are holding ourselves back.

I've even been able to verify that in government. We have a lot of government women go through the program who say, well, government has the grade system. And so I decided to go straight to some government agencies and just pose the question. And more than one male leader said, "I wish that the women would ask me for something more. I wish they would negotiate. I can't make any changes to my offer until I'm asked."

TAMMEL

So the system sounds like it's designed around knowing that women are not going to attempt to get past that barrier. And what about this concept of finding your own style of leadership. What would you say for a woman who doesn't know how to approach this?

SCHOEN

I have tapped into experts. The one on leadership and executive presence is taught by a woman named Kimberly Roush. She wrote a book called "Big: Who are you when you are big?" And it's about discovering your values when you're in your most resourceful or best self, and operating from those values.

The concept is that executive presence comes automatically when you're confident.

When you're confident, you're usually speaking from what you hold close in your heart, then you never have to lie, you never have to fake it. You never have to try to remember, "Oh, what was it that a good leader does?" It's in your heart and that automatically exudes a sort of leadership presence that is effortless.

TAMMEL

And then you mentioned the differences between men and women communication. Men often don't even ask. They just say, "Here's my number." Do you ever work with women who make that discovery?

SCHOEN

Yes, absolutely. One of the experts is Katerina Hankova. She is a financial planner. She has for years been teaching women how to negotiate compensation. She really does teach the women how to do what you're saying: "This is my number. This is what I'm looking for."

She not only teaches them that, but she teaches them all the different areas that they can negotiate. One step further, Anne, is she basically says you have to negotiate, even if you're happy with the number, because they will judge what kind of professional and person you are based on whether you negotiate.

I even had a CEO of one of our funders say to me — a female CEO of a huge engineering firm, "I'm to the point now where if they don't negotiate on salary, I may not hire them, because what that's showing me is they're not going to negotiate well for our company."

So it's a job skill, in addition to being a personal advocacy skill.

TAMMEL

Isn't it that a lot of women don't realize this, and they feel like we're raised to not be too pushy? How do they find that middle ground where they can just confidently discover their values and state their worth?

SCHOEN

That brings into play something that we study in our male female work culture workshop, and that is the double bind. And the double bind doesn't exist for men and exists in a very real way for women, and what it says is that likability and competence are negatively correlated for women. So if you're too bold and too confident, then people see you as harsh or overbearing, something negative, whereas they would characterize a man as a great leader, bold. And then if she's too nice, then they may see her as a doormat and not as competent. I've actually suffered from this in my career at different points in time where I didn't realize until hindsight that people maybe didn't see me as competent as I was because I was being so nice.

It's something women have to deal with. It is a very fine line. When women cross over into more of what we consider the male's realm of leading a business, it's not as readily accepted. So we do teach women that it does exist and to sort of dip their toe in the water gingerly and note the response to try to figure out where that line of acceptable behavior is, because unfortunately, it's different for every sector of business and every group of people. It's one of the challenges, one of the dances that women have to do to succeed, unfortunately. But we're honest about that.

TAMMEL

How about your program in general—what's the structure and the timeframe and the coaching aspect?

SCHOEN

It's a year-long program, and the workshops are intensive—three hours, once a month for eight months.

We do it once a month for a couple of reasons. A lot of our corporate employers aren't willing to let their employees go for such a long period of time more than once a month. But the other thing is, we're getting into some heavy duty data and information that requires behavioral change, and that is not always easy. It takes effort, it takes awareness, it takes observation. So what we're trying to do is give the women time to execute and to really give things thought and try to put them into practice before we pile on another principle for them to employ.

After the eight months is over, we have graduation, and then they go into the coaching portion of the program. That's about a three-month period over the summer time, and they get five one-on-one coaching sessions that's currently funded through a grant through Chapman University, and that makes a full year.

TAMMEL

I'd love to hear about what you have found incorporating this coaching element. What difference does it make?

SCHOEN

Everybody gets something different out of coaching, but it's all very personal. Only we know what we continue to struggle with in our lives. There are some coaches that are very familiar with this curriculum, so when someone coaches with them, they can help them implement the principles we're teaching. But that's not the direction everybody goes with the coaching. Some of them want to learn how to implement some of the things they're learning. Some of them have more deeply rooted, recurring types of things that are happening to them that really take some internal questioning and investigation.

I think the beauty of it is that the client drives it. The coaches ask, "What do you want to work on? What's your biggest struggle?" And from that stems the work. And my hope is that many of them will continue their coaching journey past the period of time that we're funding. I've had a coach for 30 years. I would never be without one. And we tell them, "You are the most important and impactful money-making tool that you have. You must invest in it."

TAMMEL

Once you realize the value of transformative coaching, and that concept of as a leader, finding that state where you realize, "Oh, I'm my most valuable commodity."

SCHOEN

Here's another thing we say to them when we first start. We have an orientation, and I ask, "How many of you want to be at the top of your game? You want to reach the top. You want to win."

Usually, a majority raise their hand. And then I say to them, "If you think about it, there's probably not an athlete in the world that would aspire to be the best in their sport and not have a coach.

So why would we aspire to be the best at anything and not have a coach?" It's a best practice. If that's truly what you want, you have to have a coach.

TAMMEL

Starting internally, starting within, starting with your mindset. Doesn't everything flow out of that?

SCHOEN

Yes, absolutely, not just physical conditioning. Sometimes it's the mind work, even for athletes.

TAMMEL

What about women who know something deep down, knows, "Okay, I'm driven to this. I'm meant for this," but the world's just not jiving with it?

SCHOEN

Throughout the course of the Women Rising Leadership Academy through those eight months, there's transformation. Women come to understand is that nobody will see you as a leader if you don't see yourself as a leader. There's some things you need to understand and work on, like speaking from your values, so that you have executive presence.

On mindset, I teach them, you must always treat everybody around you as a client, including your boss. Your boss is your client. Anybody who's giving you money for anything, they're your customer. So if you approach it that way, that's almost a personal branding issue.

You can't, unless you're in a toxic environment, it's hard to lose with that service mindset or that service mentality, because you're not doing it for someone else, you're actually doing it for yourself. And that's transformative.

A lot of women come back, and they will say, "My boss was asking, 'What's up with Sierra? How come she seems like a whole different person?'"

It's not just one workshop or one message that does it, but all of them put together over time with the factual data about what leadership is and how it needs to come authentically or you just won't be successful.

TAMMEL

How often does a woman need to leave the environment she's comfortable in start her own in order to make that a reality?

SCHOEN

If you love what you're doing and your values align with leadership, you're probably in the right place, unless you're hitting a brick wall on compensation or opportunity.

Sometimes they want to go do their own thing. And sometimes they need to go to a different organization.

I never wanted to do anything different when I quit my job. I could tell that no matter what I did, people were having a hard time seeing me the way I needed them to see me. So I left.

I will ask: is the problem only your boss, or does the problem go several steps above you? If it's systemic, if it goes all the way to the top, you're probably not going to change it.

But if you're just waiting out a boss, build relationships

around that person and see if you can have an impact. And then sometimes it's just time to leave.

TAMMEL

Once we get comfortable taking up that space, sometimes we do need to take up greater spaces. Sometimes we need to create our own.

SCHOEN

Well, the principles are the same. You're not going to be successful if you're not adding value to someone else in the world. So where are you going to add value in the world? What's your unique brand of adding value? And that could be through a company, and it could be through a business, but I'm a firm believer that if you're in service and you're actually solving a problem or fulfilling a need, you'll never have to worry. It's just to figure out, how do you do that? How do you want to do that?

TAMMEL

Are there any other topics that you focus on during those eight months?

SCHOEN

We start with an orientation on the status of women in the workforce.

The second one is we have an executive women's panel. It's all CEOs of different cultures and races that have made it to the top who have overcome significant bias and barriers. And that second workshop is really powerful. There are some women that go out and get promoted right after that, because they go, "Oh my gosh, I'm not alone. Everybody's experiencing this. You can overcome it."

Then the third one is the executive presence with Kimberly Roush. The fourth is salary and compensation negotiation with Katerina Hankova. I teach the next two, which are how to increase your influence, based on my book, Advancing Through Influence. And then the sixth one is the male female work culture differences. And then we go on to an alumni panel, which is women who have graduated from the program and have implemented what they learned and been promoted. And then at the very end, the last one is a graduation, and we have a brief what we call Workplace 101—the soft skills of being a very successful professional, things like mindset, things like having a service heart.

I wrote a book on influence. So I teach them how to influence people that may or may not be responding to them, how to overcome roadblocks. Because isn't it true, Anne, that everybody's not going to like us. So how do you get past those people? Are you going to quit your job every time someone doesn't like you? You can't do that. So it's a journey to get to that point. But I think most women who want to be on a leadership journey definitely leave understanding they're capable, even if they have some choices to make.

TAMMEL

The face of leadership for women is changing. It's more about women empowering women. You see this awareness and wisdom that when we come together with our greatest strengths, that's where we all excel. Can you talk about the changing face of women leadership?

SCHOEN

I think it's still changing. I think what you're talking about is more prevalent with business owners, because it is not for the faint of heart to run your own business. Your back's completely up against the wall all the time, and another business owner who's female is probably not going to be offended if you speak strongly about something.

Still, in corporate America, it is not uncommon for a woman to leave because her boss is too harsh, not really realizing that had that been a man, probably would have been okay.

So I think there's still work to do in our organizations, but when it comes to entrepreneurs, I think there's a lot more slack, because we need that support system of each other. I try to get that message out there: don't be the woman that thinks harshly about a woman just because she spoke boldly.

Don't be the woman that gets a position and then doesn't look behind you to see how you can help the next person.

Be the person that's going to make the change that we all want to see, and together, we'll be a lot stronger.

Men have the good old boys club. It's not a bad thing for the men.

So why don't we have the good old girls club?

Why don't we give each other a leg up?

Why don't we sponsor each other?

TAMMEL

And how about what you are doing currently to educate executive leaders?

SCHOEN

We're just branching out into that territory. We had a big success. We used the Brea Chamber and our business owners, a mixed crowd, to do a very abbreviated version for International Women's Day, and the men were coming up and saying, "Oh my gosh, I had no idea. I want to know more. This is crazy," and that was maybe about 20% of the information that we have in our full workshop.

So I'm currently working on retooling that for a mixed crowd consumption.

And we have a couple of companies, one of them a construction company—which is historically not so great for women—a CEO who's willing to be a pilot to help me come in and train their C-suite executives. I also did this with Mercury Insurance, and it went really well there too.

So before the end of the year, we'll be rolling out our C-suite training or HR training to see if we can start educating on the other side of organizations about some of these principles and facts that can help them be more profitable.

TAMMEL

As we close our conversation, where are you going with WRLA, and what can we watch for?

SCHOEN

Thank you for asking. We're going to continue to grow the face-to-face program. I can see us having more than one cohort a year at some point. We did get a grant from Chevron this year to bring the program online, so we will be filming all our workshops and creating an online version next year. I'm a firm believer in the face-to-face. But we really want WRLA to be accessible across the United States and even in other countries if people so desire.

There are other chambers that are interested in having it as a workforce development program. So I think our focus with our advisory board, and certainly mine, is now that we know it works, how many people can we get it to, and then also augmenting with that corporate training—how do we take care of the awareness on the other side of things, so that women have more hands reaching down to help them as well?

TAMMEL

The Women Rising Leadership Academy is expanding, and you've shared that you want it accessible across the United States and even in other countries. The challenges you've identified — internal barriers, external barriers, the research on why women aren't reaching the top — are not unique to the United States. What would it look like to bring this framework to women leaders in other countries and cultures?

SCHOEN

The Women Rising Leadership Academy will be online by the end of 2026 and will be accessible across the United States and other countries. This will give women across the country and the world an opportunity to learn about bias, barriers and solutions, and to apply them in their specific situations. The program includes virtual live question and answer events, so members of the Academy will have access to personalized coaching relative to their needs. It's an exciting development that will help women everywhere.

BOARDVANCE AND WOMEN'S INFLUENCE
IN CONVERSATION WITH DITA SHEMKE

I first met Dita Shemke at The Park Club during a Success with Purpose gathering. After a few conversations, it became clear we share a love of Italy, cooking, and celebrating *la dolce vita*. More importantly, we share a belief that women belong at the center of structural decision-making.

Dita founded Boardvance because she saw a pattern. Talented women build careers, earn credentials, complete board readiness programs—and then stall. Somewhere between qualification and appointment, momentum slows. Dita calls that gap the "last mile." It can take years to cross. Few address it directly.

When Dita chaired the Orange County campaign for 50/50 Women on Boards in 2019, she saw advocacy working—awareness was rising, but pathway clarity was not. Women had résumés and certificates, but they lacked a structured bridge to their first corporate board seat.

Dita founded Boardvance as the answer. The model is deliberately small: cohort-based, hands-on, accountability-driven. It focuses on positioning, preparation, access, and sustained support—not simply credentials.

What Dita has built is not simply a program. It is an architectural intervention. She identified the invisible drop-off point—the space between qualification and placement—then designed a structure that carries women across it.

In Silicon Valley we talk about closing execution gaps and reducing friction in systems. Boardvance does precisely that, but in governance.

In our dialogue, Dita emphasizes one point: board service is influence. It shapes policy, it shapes culture, and it shapes capital allocation.

When you change who sits at the table, you change what gets funded, what gets built, and how decisions are made. The "last mile" is rarely about talent. It is about access, sponsorship, and structure. Dita chose to build that structure.

ANNE TAMMEL

Dita, can we start with your roots? How did your upbringing shape the woman you are today?

DITA SHEMKE

I was born in the Philippines, and my family was above middle class. My dad was the only breadwinner for eight kids, and we were all able to go to private schools. We had maids in the house, a car — it was pretty lucky to have that kind of a setup.

My dad was the first in his family to have a degree. He was a civil engineer and an artist. My mom was a nurse, brought up by her aunt who had means, so she never wanted for anything.

Her last name is French — Fonacier. Anybody you meet who's Filipino with that last name is related to me!

The story goes, the very first Fonacier in the Philippines was a soldier in the French army who was Basque.

My version of the story was he probably crossed the Pyrenees from France to Spain, jumped in a galleon that took him to the Philippines.

That's my version of how my first known maternal ancestor got there.

TAMMEL

What inspired you to bring humans together in a unique way—and how do you see us coming together when women finally inhabit this space we're meant to inhabit?

SHEMKE

Collaboration speaks volumes to me. Everybody has a talent they bring to the table. It's inefficient and largely ineffective when people work in silos, because then you don't give the opportunity for others to really enjoy your gifts and vice versa. To be a great leader, you have to be open to different points of view, and there's no way you can have all the answers. Especially in today's world where things are changing so fast.

Helping women succeed has always been a big deal for me. That stems from my own personal experience. When I was going through a divorce I had a 10-year-old son and I had a new job and I had a female boss and she said to me, "If you're going through a divorce, aren't you supposed to speak to an attorney?" I was divorcing my ex-husband who was a lawyer. I said, "Yeah, but I don't know anybody."

She said to me, "There's a women's center at UCI, go over there and check it out." So I did. The class was called the Legal Aspects of Divorce. I sat there in the room and there were a few women there. They all had the same stories.

The younger women said, "I didn't have any career, didn't have a job. I have young children. When I got married, I decided to just stay home and take care of the children and my husband decided, 'I don't want this responsibility anymore.' He upped and left me with the kids. I have no means of supporting myself."

The older women, their story was, "I postponed my career to take care of my children. When they have grown and left the nest, my husband decided it's time for him to also find a younger version of me. Here I am left without any means of supporting myself."

I remember thinking, "Oh my God, how lucky am I? I have a job that can financially support me. I don't have to worry about just settling. I actually have power." That's when I said to myself, "If I can make at least one other woman feel this way, how great would that be?"

Therein was the beginning of my passion for helping women become self-sufficient.

TAMMEL

When you say you realized you had power — that you didn't have to settle — that feels like a turning point. What year was this?

SHEMKE

Late eighties. My female boss and I decided we were going to start a women's group at work. I worked for an R&D company where a lot of women worked. Photographers, artists, writers. She said, "We should band together." She took me under her wing. She was a mentor for me.

Then I started volunteering to help women put business

plans together and anything related to women and financial independence.

I happened to work for this manufacturing company and they kept reasoning I couldn't be promoted to manager of financial analysis because I didn't have an MBA. I said, "Okay, I'll show you." I happened to be working with the director of HR — we'd been doing workshops together for the production people. He was going through a Presidential Key Executive program at Claremont. Peter Drucker was his advisor. He said, "Leave it up to me. I'll run it up the flagpole." I was accepted into the executive MBA program at Pepperdine and that opened up so much for me. It helped me understand myself better, my capabilities, the things that I want to do in life.

Then that company went through a leveraged buyout and my position changed. Maybe it was bravado—I decided to start my own business. I did a couple of startups. My last startup, we had a fiber optic technology that we patented. Our first customer was Disney and other big names in the industry followed. But then my partner wanted to take the business in a different direction. We parted ways which freed me up to do what I'm doing today.

In B-school, I had a study buddy who kept saying "Dita, you would be a great financial advisor. You have the demeanor. You have the experience, the training. You have a very calming effect on people."

One day I opened the Wall Street Journal and there is this full page ad for Smith Barney looking for female financial advisors. Three months later, after interviews with several people, they offered me the job. I said, "You don't understand. I'm still not convinced this is what I want to do." In my mind, I wanted to do management consulting. I wanted to advise companies to find solutions to problems and help them grow.

Then the person who hired me said, "Let me put it this way. I give you a salary, everything you need—certifications and training - to go into production. If after six months you don't like it, you can walk away and owe me nothing. Will you take the job?"

I called my trusted advisors and they all said to me, "Are you nuts? You know how much you love to learn? Think of this as another MBA." That's how I approached it.

When I got started, what I wanted to do was build a business around consulting. But most of the people in my industry were traders. Nobody was talking about planning or advising. I think when you're searching and you're open, things will come to you. I received a timely invitation from a CPA introducing this senior business executive who wanted to start a group for what is now known as Vistage.

This chair not only allowed me to think outside the box and restructure my practice the way I want but he also became one of my first and most loyal clients. Today he is one of my best sources for business owner referrals. Over time, my practice has evolved into the consulting practice I once aspired to build. Working with owners of private companies, helping to quantify when and how to best monetize their ownership that aligns business with their personal goals. I've become an "informal" member of their Board of Advisors.

TAMMEL

Can you share more about Boardvance?

SHEMKE

Boardvance is the brainchild of invention. Discovery is really looking at the same thing and thinking something different.

I've been on nonprofit boards for many years and have been disappointed with the lack of commitment from some of my board member colleagues, and also the inability of the nonprofit to enforce what needs to happen in that boardroom. I said, "Okay, enough of that. My time is valuable. I have talents, gifts, and ideas that I am eager to share. I want to belong on a board where I can make an impact and get compensated for my contribution."

I met Betsy Berkhemer-Credaire, who was the CEO of 20/20 Women on Boards. I chaired the Orange County campaign for 2019 at the Center Club. Over 250 people showed up. Standing room only. We invited CEOs of public companies headquartered here in Orange County to be on a panel. Sitting board directors led small group discussions sharing their personal journeys to the boardroom.

In the three years of chairing the Orange County campaign for the organization, I noticed the women - members of the leadership committee - who were helping to raise money for the organization were not being helped to achieve their own personal goal of being on a corporate board. This was the gap that I identified which later became Boardvance.

TAMMEL

You call it the "last mile." In business we talk about scaling and execution risk. What does that last mile actually look like?

SHEMKE

I say there's three phases during one's board search. Remember just over ten years ago, this was not an option for women as a career path. We don't have many role models. So first, you hear about it then you go, "That sounds like a great opportunity for me."

Phase two is when you dig deeper. Do more due diligence by networking with sitting directors and enrolling in a board readiness program to learn the basics of what it means to be on a corporate board of directors, quite different from being on a nonprofit board where the stakes, metrics and caliber of talents is quite different. With a certificate of completion on one hand and a board bio on the other you then ask yourself, "Okay, now what?"

That's where Boardvance comes in. It's the last mile. It takes up to three years for qualified female candidates to go from "now what?" to the first corporate board appointment. That's the gap Boardvance aims to fill.

There are 3,000 publicly traded companies in the United States, but 99% of businesses are privately held. In reality, your first board role is going to be with a private company. Nobody really talks about that. That's what Boardvance talks about.

We've created a Boardvance ecosystem that is made up of different components aimed to specifically address what is needed to be successful on your board journey. We've developed, tested, and delivered the Boardvance Navigator Mastermind, a proprietary program where we take you from your certificate and your board bio to advanced training, rebranded board bio and targeted networking personalized to your very own archetype. At the end you have identified companies you will be seeking for board appointments, and go through a mock interview with senior executives and independent directors on the other side of the table. Each session, you produce a deliverable to add to your personal playbook. As a Navigator Mastermind alum, you automatically become part of an Inner Circle where you receive continued accountability and support throughout your journey to your first board appointment. When you finally make that leap, you come back and you become a role model and a mentor to those still in their journey. It's circular.

TAMMEL

How does Boardvance address the fact that maybe 30% of upper level management is occupied by women, and then it becomes this funnel—and when you get to a very senior level it's maybe 3 to 5% women?

SHEMKE

If you have women in leadership positions, they have a tendency to bring other women to fill vacancies in the organization. There's all kinds of metrics that support having women at the top levels of a company, means less turnover and provides a more creative environment that ultimately translates to a better bottom line. The ultimate goal of Boardvance is to increase the pipeline for qualified women ready to fill open vacancies in the highest level, the boardroom where policy is created and implemented throughout the organization.

I believe in collaboration, with both men and women. Working in silos is proven ineffective especially in today's business environment where everything seems to change more rapidly than ever because of technology.

Creating an environment that is most conducive to learning while providing accountability and support is a huge part of the way I structured Boardvance. I used my own personal experiences in my wealth management practice and my executive education as models. Small, intimate, collaborative because women tend to do better in small learning environments.

We also recognize that women usually put themselves last. We're assigned different roles in life - mom, daughter, wife. And when each one of those roles needs us to be present, we are there! Front and center!

And when it comes time to apply for any job, women have a tendency to apply only if they feel they have met at least 85% of the qualifications.

One of the first things we tackle in the Navigator Mastermind is imposter syndrome. In our view it is important to put this in perspective before you can take a giant step toward the goal of landing your first corporate board seat.

It's huge for the women to peel off that mask before anything else!

TAMMEL

Men have it too. Though they admit it less.

SHEMKE

Adam Grant interviewed Justin Trudeau about imposter syndrome and how Justin Trudeau was worried that he will never be as good as his dad. So yes, men have it. But to your point, they're not prone to talk about it.

TAMMEL

I find it fascinating that women sometimes go out and we have to create our own version of what men have created for themselves, that we're barred from. But when we do create it, we set the future—we step into a future and we create it better.

SHEMKE

Because we look at it from a different lens. I think a wider-angle lens! It's in our DNA. We've become more inclusive because during the caveman days, men were hunters and women were gatherers. Women stayed home, took care of the children. They needed to get along with neighbors to make sure the household is in tip top shape while the guys are away. Millions of years ingrained in the way women have evolved which allows us to look at problems from a different lens.

I still say today that the way the US responded to COVID would've been totally different if we had more women in key leadership positions. Tens of thousands of lives would have been spared.

TAMMEL

Yes—in New Zealand, wasn't the woman the one leader who had it under control within a couple weeks?

SHEMKE

That's correct. But there's room for both men and women at the top. If key metrics consistently show women-led organizations have better bottom lines than their male-run counterparts shouldn't that speak volumes? What's important to note is that diverse and balanced points of view is what's needed to address all stakeholders in order for an organization to succeed. Why would a company not want to get women at that level?

I studied microfinance in Italy. There's a reason why in microfinance they focus on lending to women and their small businesses. In Africa microfinance has been successfully used to bank the unbanked - if you give money to a woman, her family benefits. And if her family benefits, it spills over to the community where schools are built. It becomes a self-enriching ecosystem. Conversely, studies have shown when men are given the money, they don't take it home. They go out and have a good time with friends. Nothing benefits the family. So this is the reason why in microfinance they work with mostly women businesses. We're collaborators. We're natural networkers. When we find something we like, we share it.

TAMMEL

When Boardvance flourishes and your vision becomes reality, how do businesses benefit and run differently?

SHEMKE

You have more diverse opinions and different ways of managing a business that takes into account all stakeholders which translates to a better bottom line. It spreads outward from employees to owners/stockholders, to the community, and eventually the world.

TAMMEL

You're launching this in Orange County. How does this vision become a model for other communities throughout the United States?

SHEMKE

This is the first one. We want to make sure we get it right. I'm already being asked about offices in other parts of the country. I need to make sure we're okay. I'm a Virgo, I like things done the right way. Quality versus quantity—quality is very important to me in enhancing value.

Once we perfect it here, there's ways to replicate it in other places. But to be able to do that you have to have quality guidelines in place. Achieving consistency in delivery and quality of the products and services you provide is key for a successful implementation elsewhere.

For me, I am creating a company with a double bottom line. I want us to make money while doing good. A model organization would be akin to Patagonia.

I really believe in the Boardvance ecosystem, where each component adds value to others in the group. Where the sum of the parts is greater than the whole. When Boardvance members land that coveted first board seat, they have a chance to come back and become role models and mentors. It's a close-loop community that helps each member become successful regardless of where you are in your journey.

TAMMEL

What's our vision for this community? And how are we contributing to that vision as the leaders of this community?

SHEMKE

In business we have KPIs and we need to also use that in the nonprofit world, but you have to add the other component to it. How do you measure impact?

There are two organizations that I believe embody the important elements of how organizations can do business while doing good. Movements like these are going to create the kind of environment where it's not just about making money - it's also about making the community a better place for everyone.

It will be tremendous if we can emulate their practices and systems to benefit our local community.

GIIN, the Global Impact Investment Network - thegiin.org - a leading industry body for impact investing dedicated to increasing its scale and effectiveness around the world.

Conscious Capitalism - consciouscapitalism.org - a global organization dedicated to transforming business by promoting a "higher purpose" beyond just profit.

TAMMEL

It takes visionaries who believe these visions can come true and the thought leaders willing to do the work.

SHEMKE

Being a visionary means being willing to go beyond the obvious and be brave enough to say it and do something about it.

I heard the dean of engineering at UCI speak at a TED Talk many years ago. His topic was about the future of engineering. He said, "The future engineers are not the ones that are necessarily good in math and systems. The future engineers are the creative ones who can problem solve, who can understand interdisciplinary solutions and can reach out across the aisle to the non-geeky people."

TAMMEL

It gets back to how jazz bands form sometimes the best models for business teams. Because you bring all of these diverse viewpoints and backgrounds together, and they're all heard at some point. They're willing to hear one another and create cultures that honoring differences.

SHEMKE

As fast as technology is changing and as fast as the world is changing because we're so interconnected, you have to be nimble and agile to adapt to change. In regards to Boardvance, it's not about men versus women. It's really contributing and collaborating because it benefits everyone!

TAMMEL

The best leaders are lifelong learners, right? Continually learning and adapting and improving, remaining relevant.

SHEMKE

Every experience counts. If you go anywhere with this thought and humility about you—that you are not better than they are, and you are there to learn, and you are there to offer value—I don't know how you can go wrong.

There's a couple of sayings I subscribe to when it comes to leadership.

"When you become a leader, it's no longer about you. It's about the people you serve."

"If you want to go fast, go alone. If you want to go far, go with others." — old African proverb.

Boardvance was built on these tenets. The ecosystem we've created is proof of its importance.

CASA REGIS: GLOBAL RESIDENCY
IN CONVERSATION WITH MIKELLE STANDBRIDGE

Mikelle Standbridge has taken a building from the 1600s — a monastery abandoned for twenty years in the mountains of Piedmont, Italy — and made it breathe again. What started as one woman's instinct to bring the world to a forgotten place has become an international artist residency that draws poets, painters, opera singers, Appalachian musicians, theater artists, and writers from across the globe.

There is no electricity turned on. The only water runs from a stone fountain in the courtyard. The rooms face south and fill with natural light through windows that have no screens. It is, by every measure, a space stripped to its original bones.

That stripping is the point. What Mikelle has learned — and what I have come to understand in my own work — is that when you remove what does not belong, the core essence becomes visible. The frescoes behind the 1980s paint. The terracotta beneath the brown carpet.

Mikelle grew up in a small mountain village in Southern California, spent three years in France studying photography, moved to Italy in 2000, and lived for twenty years in the city before finding the building that would find her — a monastery with an extraordinary garden, walking distance from the weekend house she and her husband had bought in a tiny pre-Alpine village.

The building itself carries a history that mirrors what happens to the artists who come. It belonged first to a philanthropic doctor known for bringing medicine to rural communities who could not afford it. It was then donated to a religious order whose nuns opened the doors to local children and taught them French, Latin, and theater. People in the village today, in their eighties and nineties, still remember growing up with those nuns in those rooms. When Mikelle arrived, the building had been empty for two decades. She peeled back the 1970s wood paneling and found fresco ceilings. She pulled up the brown carpet and found the original terracotta. She is still finding what is underneath.

The region itself is part of the story. Piedmont — Piemonte, at the foot of the mountain — is one of Italy's most unsung landscapes: pre-Alpine villages, fluorescent green rice fields, snow-capped mountains, the Barolo wine region, and the birthplace of the slow food movement. It is an hour and a half from Milan or Turin by train, close enough to reach but quiet enough to disappear.

Mikelle does work I recognize. She creates rooms where the noise falls away, where artists who have been blocked for years suddenly find they can write again, where strangers construct an opera together on site and an audience follows them through the building, room by room, into something none of them had planned.

Kevin McGrath, who wrote the foreword to my first book, was the poet in residence at Harvard, and he wrote about Love of Place — how we fall in love with places the way we fall in love with people, because a place puts us in touch with a part of ourselves we did not know was there. That is what Casa Regis does. That is what Mikelle built.

This is a conversation about what happens when we stop long enough to hear it.

ANNE TAMMEL

Mikelle, can we start with your background and your journey to this place?

MIKELLE STANDBRIDGE

I grew up in Southern California in a very small mountain village, and I did my studies in art at San Francisco State University. The program was interdisciplinary and experimental art. In Chicago, just finished my MFA at U of

C, I ended up meeting my to-be husband who is Italian. He's from Milan.

In the year 2000 I transferred to Italy, and we lived for twenty years in Milan. But as most Milanese people do, we looked for a place for the weekends about an hour and a half outside of the city. We ended up buying a house in this little mountain village, and I found myself in the same sort of village environment in which I grew up, but after thirty-five years of living in urban spaces.

What I really found out is that these little mountain villages are full of culture. There are so many people with nonprofit associations promoting the arts, culture, dance, literature, nature walking. Within walking distance, I saw this other place that had this incredible garden and it looked somewhat abandoned. It belonged to the church and it was a monastery for nuns and had been in disuse for twenty years. I ended up creating a nonprofit association for Culture and Contemporary Art so they could donate the building to the association. We opened the doors in 2020 — during COVID, of all things.

We ended up adopting another building, Villa Emma, which is also an incredible location for retreats. So we organically started this international call for artists in residence. It's not limited to just visual artists. We welcome writers and other thinkers, people who have an interest in exploring something about this history or this location or something to do with Italy.

TAMMEL

What you built from that discovery is extraordinary — you're bringing together so many disciplines in one space. Theater, poetry, music, visual art — a Black Mountain College or a Laurel Canyon, where creative spirits gather in nature to create. What happens when all of those disciplines come together under one roof?

STANDBRIDGE

During one recent retreat, there was a theater person and a writer. The writer wanted to write her own play but didn't know how to put it in play format. The theater artist had new poetry that needed editing. The writer edited her poetry and the theater artist helped put her book into theater format. They're looking to produce that piece together when they get back to England.

Another group had an opera singer accompanied by Appalachian musicians and visual artists, and they put on this piece with intense contemporary opera. The visual artists were painting all over themselves and the canvases as a performance to the meaning of the lyrics. It ended up being a complete stage performance. They moved around the building so the audience followed them into different rooms.

I've had people from the audience come back years later and tell me they've never had such an intense experience.

Those artists had never worked together previously. It was a new piece they constructed on site and for the site.

TAMMEL

What you've built — and are continuing to build — will be valuable to people across the globe searching for better ways to collaborate. What do you see happening when global perspectives meet in a place that invites true collaboration?

STANDBRIDGE

I can answer from personal experience. I headed up an artist residency in China, after working closely with a Chinese curator who held two exhibitions at Casa Regis. She organized that other fellow Chinese artists would host us once there, and we were invited to give workshops to their photo societies on our techniques. There was myself and two other artists.

This was followed up by an invitation to the Chinese photographers to come stay with us in Italy, where they also gave workshops and interpreted the local life and landscape.

Working with this group, I have never had so many stereotypes just disintegrate into thin air so fast. Even if all through Google Translate and translators, we communicated so well, learned so much about each other's country, and truly created lifelong friendships. Laughing, eating, going on excursions every day.

We followed up with an exhibition of their work created here, and they followed up with an exhibition of our work, interpreting China. For me as an artist, as a host, as a sustainer of cultural exchanges, it just doesn't get any richer.

Something that has surprised me and was completely unexpected as I took on the enterprise of Casa Regis was that I moved seamlessly from being just an artist, to an organizer, to a leader, even to becoming a mentor. I help multiple local artists develop their careers and from the local university, I have three international interns — from Russia and Kazakhstan — getting credit and managerial experience for their Cultural Heritage degree.

We have become a team and they help me as much as I help them.

TAMMEL

What you're describing — artists who've never met, constructing something together in a matter of days — that doesn't happen in most environments. I work with CEOs and senior executives who spend millions trying to get their teams to collaborate at that level, and most never get close. There's something about stripping away the noise that unlocks it. Was that your intention for this space, or did the space itself create the conditions?

STANDBRIDGE

Casa Regis is this building from the 1600s, and there are two things that I like about it. One is its own history because it belonged to a philanthropic doctor known for bringing medication out to the population, especially in rural areas where they couldn't afford it. So there was already this legacy of somebody with something to offer, connecting it to the community.

The building was donated to one of their granddaughters and she brought it to the nunnery. These nuns opened the doors to all the local children and taught them French, Latin, and even theater. People around here today in their eighties or nineties remember having grown up with these nuns in this location. There was this opening up to the community.

When I showed up, it's a different world — it's contemporary art — but I felt it remained in the legacy of opening this location to the world.

This building's from the 1600s and I do have electricity, but I basically never turn it on. The only water is from the running water in the fountain in the courtyard. Artists sleep at our house which is a normal house with water and heat. But when they're at Casa Regis to work on their art, we use all natural light because the building was designed to face south. Every room has windows facing the garden. You can go in the garden and get incredible drinking water. The space is naturally lit, there's no screens on the windows. It's open and grounded, and you feel the history of these super thick walls and fresco ceilings. We are in a mountain village, so it is fresh air and sometimes you hear animals outside. There's a homemade cheese store right down the road.

I keep the space very simple, very minimalist. If someone needs a table we give them a table and a chair, otherwise the rooms are open. Most people live in very crowded spaces. When you get to this clean slate, clean air and fresh water, you can hear the fountain running. It's an incredible creative space.

TAMMEL

The way you describe that space — clean slate, clean air, the fountain running — it's a world apart from where most of us operate. I've passed through Piedmont but never truly stopped and spent time. Every time I encounter a wine or a cheese from Piemonte, it stays with me. Tell me more about the region.

STANDBRIDGE

Piemonte literally means at the foot of a mountain. We're in the pre-Alps area. It's a region not particularly known to most tourism, which is greatly to our advantage because it's very accessible. There aren't crowds. It's gorgeous. It's one of the most unsung unknown areas of Italy, with incredible mountain views.

We're an hour and a half drive or train to Turin or Milan. Turin has incredible museums and was central to the Savoia Dynasty, one of the longest lasting dynasties ever. There are castles turned into contemporary art museums. And in lower Piedmont there's a huge wine region where Barolo comes from, some of Italy's most famous wine.

The slow food movement started there as well, in the seventies when the first McDonald's showed up. Somebody wanted to counterbalance it with slow food. Restaurants will have a sticker in their window if they're part of the movement where they try to do zero kilometer buying and have as much local supplies as possible. It's about good eating and making choices about what you financially support. What you're eating is a way of making a political decision.

When you're driving from Milan up to Piedmont, there are these moments when there's this fluorescent green, which is the rice fields, and then the mountains, snow capped. They're breathtaking. Arborio is the name of a risotto rice, and that's the name of a small town here. So the rice is named after the town itself.

Villa Emma is in a different valley. It was built in 1893 when they just had donkeys and horses. American guest architects have said they don't know how they built such quality and massive stone structures, with no trucks to transport the materials up the steep hills. That valley has small towns that have won being among the top cutest in all of Italy and incredible locations with glacier-cold rivers where all of my guests love to jump in. They all claim to have been reborn. The water is so crisp, fresh and energizing.

TAMMEL

The building itself is a metaphor for the creative spirits drawn to it — removing all the wrong carpet to find frescoes and terracotta underneath. The women I work with through programs like SoCal Women in Business face something similar. So much of what makes us extraordinary has been forgotten by years of corporate conditioning or covered by the noise of other people's expectations. We need a space that strips all of that away. How does this show up with artists who come to you?

STANDBRIDGE

There's an English artist, Alice Shepherd Fiddler, who stayed for a month. She had the goal of just listening to the building, responding to the building and local materials.

The way we welcomed her, we invited local musicians and closed all the windows. It was the three of them in the rooms in the dark. The musicians just had a spoon or a stick and they moved around tapping and touching things. Each room clearly had something to say. These voices came out, these animated things. I'd never seen anything like it.

They would do one room and close it, then move to the next room. The next room had a completely different sound, a completely different response. They did the whole building like that as if it was an encountering of the spirits.

But there was this little room off to the side of the courtyard and Alice said, I bet if I get every chair in this whole building and line them all up in this room, they'll all fit perfectly. And she did. And it did. They were all set perfectly in order, four across, six long.

Then this woman came to visit the show. She had studied with the nuns when she was little. She said: *we used to sit like that in that room for catechism, lined up exactly like that, facing where the nun would have been.*

So even though it was just a storage room, when Alice came she turned it into this little mini classroom where all these different chairs were like different eras and different bodies.

Some were from the fifties, some from the 1900s. Some were wood, some were metal, clearly a classroom chair. Some were wicker, clearly a garden chair. It was like all of these chairs were eras and people and souls.

In Alice's perception of the building, she had actually tapped into some kind of pre-moment before she got there.

TAMMEL

Kevin McGrath wrote about this — Love of Place. How we fall in love with places as much as people, because a place puts us in touch with a part of ourselves we didn't know was there.

What Alice found in that room — what those walls were holding — sounds like love left by previous spirits.

STANDBRIDGE

When they did this spoon talking to the rooms, one room was actually like painful sounds coming out. Like suffering. Clearly there was a lot of pent up stuff in that room.

I was thinking about the history because the life of a woman, even if part of a middle, upper class doctor's family, she still would have been extremely limited. What if there had been wives and sisters and mothers who couldn't get out what they wanted? What if they had the capacity, but not the role in society that permitted their say?

And then I thought about the nuns because there was a period when the Veneto region had floods and food shortage, and when many moved to Piedmont looking for work. If you were a young girl that had lost her family or didn't have a place to go, they'd put you with the nuns. Sometimes it was permanent, sometimes not, but they weren't necessarily religious choices made because of faith. They were economic choices. If you came as the poorest member of a convent, you were the one doing the cleaning, the cooking, the lower end jobs. Probably not allowed to have boyfriends, experiment with growing up. So I thought there might have been a lot of suffering.

Mattea Gernentz, an American poet living in Edinburgh, stayed with us just a week, but wrote a beautiful poem which captured what I thought those women might be feeling. I thought she did a wonderful job of bringing out what those walls might have been saying.

TAMMEL

I look forward to planning Poets and Dreamers retreats in that space. The term itself has its own calling — Lady Gregory introduced it in 1903 for people who were thinking differently, living differently, daring to imagine what others would not. Kevin McGrath kept encouraging me to grow Poets and Dreamers because it truly is for everyone. This space was waiting for exactly that kind of spirit.

STANDBRIDGE

It's rewarding to have a place where you can invite people to do that. I also work on promoting the artists outside of this small village. They might come here for a retreat experience, but I stay in contact with gallery connections in Los Angeles and internationally.

Several of my artists have traveled to galleries in Milan, Paris, and China, so we work on sharing internationally what we've been able to produce here. It's a place we keep connected to continuing possibilities.

TAMMEL

What you've built is a space where the noise falls away and what was always there becomes audible.

Every leader I've worked with, every woman building something that matters, whether they have the time to explore it, at some point is searching for that.

The voice beneath the noise. It was always there...

PARIS, ART, AND ARCHITECTURE
IN CONVERSATION WITH MICHÈLE DAGHER
FATTAL

Michèle Dagher Fattal is a Parisian-based supervision-level coach who has devoted her career to integrating art and creativity into her practice. Having met Michèle through Damian Goldvarg's coaching program, and having woven metaphors into my own practice—which also relies on neuroscience and vision boards—I was enchanted to learn more about her unique approach.

Michèle has crafted this innovative style of coaching, deeply influenced by her father's background as an architect and a childhood steeped in beauty, aesthetics, and artistic expression. In this conversation, we explore how her practice taps into the transformative power of creativity in coaching and leadership. By integrating visual metaphors, drawing, and the creative process, Michèle's coaching model delivers solutions traditional methods sometimes overlook. Her philosophy treats creativity not simply as an add-on but a foundational pathway toward deeper human connection, insight, and powerful problem-solving.

Through our dialogue, Michèle reveals how art acts as a universal language to transcend cultural differences, empowering clients to access unconscious wisdom and arrive at unexpected solutions. From vision boards that manifest ambitious goals to collaborative creative processes that unify, Michèle invites each of us—in a world increasingly focused on speed and analytical thinking—to pause, step back, and step into the transformative act of creating something beautiful.

ANNE TAMMEL

Michèle, in my own practice with leaders, I've integrated metaphor and visual thinking. So I am genuinely intrigued by yours. How did your background lead you here, and how did creativity become central to your practice?

MICHÈLE DAGHER FATTAL

I grew up in an artistic and creative environment. My father was an architect who loved beauty. This aesthetic value was very important for all of us. I began my professional life teaching. Art and creativity have always been in my journey.

Then I had to leave my country because of the war—I'm Lebanese. I came to Paris and worked for an antique dealer.

When my first child was born, the first thing my dad told me was: if you have to teach something to your children, teach them beauty. It is always there.

Every time I do something, I try to make it beautiful.

I can't imagine my life without beauty, without nature, without creativity, and it's part of my professional life—I use art in my coaching practice.

TAMMEL

I work with executives who are often trapped in analytical thinking—spreadsheets, metrics, strategic plans. What I've found is that the breakthrough comes when we shift modalities. How do you use art and creativity in your practice?

FATTAL

My coaching practice uses art and creativity through images as support. I can use images, environment, movies, music. I can ask my client to draw—drawing, writing, painting, modeling are powerful tools to take a breath, move and let the brain process in its own rhythm.

During our conversation, sometimes a word comes to mind, sometimes I need to draw something and give it back to my client, which can help them move forward and have an insight.

TAMMEL

This is exactly what I teach in my leadership work—that creativity isn't separate from strategy, it's the pathway to better strategy. Your clients tap into their creative spirit for problem-solving?

FATTAL

I always tell them, you don't need to know how to draw. Just follow your intuition, follow the flow. Something will emerge—an answer, an insight, a solution. It's a path from the question to the solution.

TAMMEL

In CEO circles, I've seen this repeatedly—the solution emerges when leaders stop forcing it. They step back and find a different way?

FATTAL

An image is a way to step back. I ask: What is the issue you want to work on today? If you put an image on it, what would it be? And then what do you want it to be at the end of our session?

From one drawing to another follows like a roadmap and they get what they want. It's very intuitive, very organic.

TAMMEL

This sounds very entrepreneurial—stepping back, seeing differently, creating their own path. In strategic planning, we call that gap analysis—but you're doing it with a paintbrush.

FATTAL

I believe in it. Some entrepreneurs are ready to slow down and explore things in a new way. I'm creative myself, an artist, and I've been living this in my own path and with all the clients I've helped.

TAMMEL

I've noticed founders who built something from nothing respond more readily to this kind of creative process. It's the executives who've spent decades inside systems— where every decision requires a deck and a data set—who pause and question it.

FATTAL

There are three ways to use art: support, making art, and feedback.

First is support—I suggest images to clients: art pieces, nature images, anything. Your issue looks like what if you choose an image? Classical music brings up images too. It's a way to step back, feel new emotions, look with a new eye. When you interact with artwork, there's an aha moment where you see the world in a new way, or you look at a problem differently because art lets you express things you couldn't before. You bring what's hidden to be visible. This brings needed information and awareness.

The second way is making art—I ask them to draw, paint. In workshops, I give them time for creativity. The third is feedback—I give feedback using my own drawings, words that pop up while we talk. This can be very awakening because it comes from somewhere else.

TAMMEL

You're creating a visual mirror for the client. I use neuroscience and metaphor in a similar way. How often do clients reach that stage where they leave the problem behind?

FATTAL

Very often, and I'm always surprised. Before our meeting today, I had a client who asked to be creative. After drawing and playing with space, he left his anxiety and feeling of being overwhelmed. He said, "I will allow life to come in and do what it can do"—in 30 minutes.

I never know how art will be part of our sessions. It comes intuitively. I suggest what comes to mind and it's always amazing.

I worked with a woman contracted for eight sessions. After three sessions, she wrote saying "everything's okay, I feel great, I'm in paradise."

It's about connection—meeting clients where they need to be met. Our role is to be present, curious, listening to what's unsaid more than what's said. Make them feel they matter. Art is a good way to connect, get self-confidence, stay calm.

TAMMEL

That phrase—"listening to what's unsaid"—is one of the most important skills in leadership. Most executives I work with are surrounded by people telling them what they want to hear. The unsaid is where the real information lives. What you've found is a way to make the unsaid visible.

FATTAL

He becomes the creator and architect of his own future. My brother is an architect, and we do similar things. He considers his client's whole environment—how they want to live.

When I'm with a client, I consider their beliefs, sensibility, how they like our conversation. With all those elements, I try to create the most suitable thing for my client. I serve them creatively without losing my identity. We co-create together.

TAMMEL

That word architect keeps surfacing. Your father was an architect. Your brother is an architect. And what you're doing is architecture—designing the interior structure of a person's next chapter. In my work building global communities, I've seen how art transcends cultural barriers. When you connect through art, you rise above differences.

FATTAL

Those things disappear. With art, you can understand each other with a drawing, a painting, a symbol. You overcome cultural differences. Art speaks to everyone. It gives sense to things, makes emotions concrete. I believe in its power —it's universal.

TAMMEL

In my work with global leaders, language can divide. Strategy decks can divide. But when you put people in a room and ask them to create something together—a vision, an image, a shared language—the walls come down.

FATTAL

First, write it down—a first step to reality.

Then draw it, or cut images that catch your eyes, stick them on paper, add words, drawings. Represent your vision, then step back and see what to add.

I need to show you my vision board. It's come true because I love it. It's my way of looking at coaching and life. It's real, so I look at it to remember. I can see what I've achieved since I made it, where I am today.

TAMMEL

I've used vision boards throughout my career—from my early days in Silicon Valley to building leadership cultures. Many of mine have been actualized. You set down something that seems impossible, but you dare to believe it can become part of your life.

FATTAL

Deep inside, you know that it's possible and what are the steps you need to take to make it happen. Sometimes it happens in a different way, but it happens.

TAMMEL

Most of the CEOs I work with can articulate where they're going, but they mistake controlling the process for ensuring the outcome. Sometimes you need to let go of the process and know you're going to get there, but you can't micromanage or force every step to make sense right away.

FATTAL

You step back and when you make it, you put it, you make it concrete. You represent your vision. You don't need to force things to be. They come alone. And if it happens that you need to force something, it's a loss of energy. I don't believe we are here for that. There is something magical in art.

TAMMEL

What is it about the process of a vision board that makes it work?

FATTAL

It's not as easy as you describe it. Of course, we need to look at it every day. It's a process. Once the vision board is created, there is reflection around it. Now that I know what I want to achieve, I have to work on it. How, what do I need? Do I need the help of anyone? What is the most important thing? And what are the steps? Having this vision board helps stay focused on what I want to achieve and what are the actions I'm going to take.

They write their question, they write their dreams, they write what they want to achieve, their goal. And then put it in images. They take the time for it, the necessary time. There are images, there are words they take—they catch what calls them. There is something, you catch it, you take it, you cut it, you keep it, and you take everything you need. And then you have a big piece of paper, you can write, give a title to your goal and put all those images, connect them all together. You can add words, writings, anything you want. Everything is allowed.

It is playful. It helps slow down and calm down. It brings positive emotions. It is an appreciative tool. Being creative, you are moving, you are doing something you have never done, sharing, getting feedback. All those little things that might seem to be not important—in my eyes they are very powerful and give meaning to the goal anyone wants to achieve.

TAMMEL

The brain believes what you tell it. If you have an image every day, a visual of this is where I'm going, your brain is being told, okay, this is your reality. Glenn Fox at USC has done extraordinary research on how gratitude reshapes neural pathways. What you're describing from the creative side, the neuroscience confirms from the inside. The image changes the brain. The brain changes the behavior. I've found that collective vision boards can be powerful conduits for teams.

FATTAL

Very beautiful. You create something all together. Everyone contributes to this vision board. What happens while creating this common vision board is powerful for the team. They all contribute together, reinforcing willingness to work as a team. For me, working collectively with creativity is the most powerful tool in organizations.

TAMMEL

This is what I teach in my leadership practice: the leader's job is alignment—bringing culture together through shared purpose. Creating together achieves that faster than talking about it.

FATTAL

They create their own culture. All differences disappear when you create something in common.

With art, we rise above differences and come together. Conflict disappears. It's replaced by appreciation, co-working, co-creating, happiness. Very powerful—it improves motivation and gives impulse. Art language is very powerful.

TAMMEL

The moment you ask a team to build something together, the energy in the room transforms. What you're validating from your work in Paris is that the vision board isn't the output. The act of making it together is.

FATTAL

Imagine a team working on the same goal creatively using art—all the ideas that emerge are new. The unexpected emerges.

TAMMEL

When you have a creative environment, that's where peak performance happens. One of my clients at Google said her key to success was having fun. Taking people out of their environment, bringing them together, making sure they have fun.

FATTAL

It's fun. I believe every learning, the biggest ideas were born with fun. Think about Disney. I've seen results with myself, clients, and groups in my workshops. They come to try. After two or three hours they leave with clear ideas, new ideas, new energy. They had fun, took time for themselves, slowed down, let go what needs to go and allowed life to come in. Very powerful.

TAMMEL

There is something magical in art. It has a transformative power. This is fundamental to my philosophy—and to how I facilitate mastermind groups. Everyone is creative.

FATTAL

This is my belief. I believe that everyone is creative. Unfortunately, a lot of people have been cut somewhere from their own creativity, but it can be awakened and it can reveal with different styles. This is the great news about it. And in times like today, when everything seems to be closed, stuck, this is the perfect moment for creativity to reveal.

TAMMEL

You've described art as a universal language that rises above cultural differences. As organizations around the world search for new approaches to leadership development—and as both women and men in leadership across industries, cultures, and continents face challenges data and strategy alone cannot solve—how do you see creativity and the methods you've built in Paris reaching leaders and organizations globally?

FATTAL

For me, art is about creating a space where something true can emerge. A reflective space. A transforming space. In my work with leaders through Art & Coaching, I first offer a pause. A space where they can step out of their roles, the pressure to decide, to perform, to have the answers. Through simple creative processes, working with colors, materials, they start exploring instead of solving.

What often happens is that they access something different... something more intuitive, more honest. Sometimes something they couldn't quite name before. The act of creating has this unique capacity to make the invisible visible, and to bring into awareness what was not yet conscious. Creativity helps reconnect with positive emotion. It reduces stress and its impact. It brings people back into the present moment.

What I find very powerful is that this goes beyond culture. I see it again and again. That moment when someone reconnects to their intuition, their inner self, or sees their situation differently. It's something very human.

So when I think about bringing this work to leaders globally, I don't think of it as exporting a method. It's more about creating the right conditions. Spaces where reflection, emotion, sensation, intuition, and exploration are allowed. And that can exist anywhere, while still respecting each culture.

Today, leaders are dealing with uncertainty and complexity that data and strategy alone can't always address. I believe creativity brings something essential. More awareness, more perspective, and a different way to navigate these challenging times.

TAMMEL

You also offer programs online that leaders around the world can access. What do those look like?

FATTAL

Yes, I do offer online programs, and for me it was important that they are not just a digital version of what I do in person.

What I try to recreate online is the same quality of space. Something opening, reflective, and engaging. Even at a distance, I invite participants to slow down, to step out of their usual environment, and to enter a more reflective, introspective process.

The formats vary. It can be individual sessions, group programs or programs for teams. But the essence remains the same.

I guide participants through simple creative explorations, using materials they have at home, combined with coaching, mentoring or supervision.

It's not about artistic skill. It's really about the experience and what emerges from it.

What I've observed is that working online can even deepen certain things. People are in their own space, which can create a different kind of intimacy and honesty.

And it also makes this work accessible to leaders in different parts of the world, with different contexts.

In person or online, it's about the quality of being, the deep presence, the intention, and the space we co-create.

TAMMEL

I've worked with executives who haven't drawn a picture or written a poem since childhood—but when they give themselves permission, something unlocks. Organizations don't just need creative solutions. They need leaders who have reconnected with their own creative instincts. That's what you're restoring in people.

FATTAL

This is what I told my brother—we do the same thing. When you look at your client, you have information to help them achieve their goal, but everything comes from them. They give you information naturally. This is why I love working with this tool. My client matters and can feel it.

TAMMEL

A painter told me his purpose was creating something beautiful that he wanted to see. Amy Winehouse said no one was creating the music she wanted to hear, so she made it herself. That's what creative spirits do as leaders— we create organizations, culture, society, a better world.

FATTAL

We can design and create it the way we want it to be. We are here for that. There are a million ways to create— poetry, writing, drawing, painting, but also gardening, cooking, dancing. Everyone is creative and everyone may use their creativity in service of a better world.

TAMMEL

Your father was an architect. How did that shape you?

FATTAL

When my first child was born, he told me, if you have something to teach your children, teach them about beauty.

TAMMEL

Now you're teaching the world about beauty—that it's still possible no matter what we're going through. We can always find beauty and create it.

FATTAL

Beauty is everywhere every day. We just need to open our eyes.

TAMMEL

I read recently that love can be considered a business strategy–and that basically love, empathy, and humanity drive better business outcomes than any profit-first model.

What you and I are both saying is that love isn't separate from the work. Love is the most powerful force in the universe. That's what drives this work—for both of us.

FATTAL

Creativity and helping people connect with their own creativity connects them to life, to the essence of life and to love. And what do we need more? The reason we are here. It's a beautiful experience because when you've experienced it, everything disappears for beautiful things. Love is the most powerful thing. I remember I ran a workshop for ICF about art in coaching. I ended with the Beatles song "Love." When we listen to it, it's very powerful.

POWER OF THE PACK
IN CONVERSATION WITH STACIE SHEPARD

Across cultures and continents, leaders continue searching for models that restore balance, cooperation, and shared purpose in human systems. Sometimes those models appear in unexpected places. In the quiet observation of how living systems organize themselves—how a pack moves, protects, and supports its members—we find principles that extend far beyond the natural world and into the way human communities, organizations, and societies learn to function together.

Stacie Shepard's journey as a nonprofit founder in Southern California reveals the transformative power of one woman's determination to reshape the way an entire field thinks through unexpected setbacks. What began as a dog-walking business during the COVID-19 pandemic evolved into the Good Shepards Foundation, an organization developing a new model of support built around the natural dynamics of canine packs—one that speaks directly to collaboration, well-being, and care.

Through personal struggle and pandemic isolation, Stacie and her children discovered that dogs offer far more than companionship. Pack dynamics demonstrate a clear, repeatable model for cooperation, shared responsibility, and collective confidence—principles that resonate far beyond animal training and into the way human communities, organizations, and institutions function around the world.

One afternoon at the Park Club in Costa Mesa, Stacie and I sat by a window in the sun and talked about her path navigating the business and nonprofit worlds with determination, faith, and a multifaceted perspective at the intersection of human and organizational wellbeing. We discussed her hybrid model of training bonded packs of dogs—rather than individual therapy animals—along with parallels to equine therapy and the unexpected discovery of an approach to collaboration that speaks to leaders across disciplines.

What Stacie and her family have built points toward something much larger than a regional initiative. It offers a living example of what many leaders in these conversations have been searching for: evidence that collaboration, shared leadership, and unified purpose are instincts embedded deeply in living systems. In every healthy pack, these instincts are visible.

Her vision extends well beyond Orange County. Stacie imagines a future where the lessons of canine pack dynamics inform how communities around the world think about leadership, care, and collective wellbeing. In that sense, the lessons of the pack speak to a larger truth about leadership itself: collaboration thrives when each member understands their role within a shared purpose.

<hr>

ANNE TAMMEL

Stacie, can we hear about what inspired you to begin this journey?

STACIE SHEPARD

First, we are three things: a family, a small business, and a nonprofit. As a family we experienced real challenges in COVID. Five years ago, when my oldest Isabella was working for another dog training company, I encouraged her to branch out on her own and offered to help. I had previously practiced as a nurse before I raised children. The original concept was simple—just a dog walking service in our community.

After a couple of years, the business was thriving. My other children were getting involved and we were healing from this traumatic time. My daughter was healing faster than the rest of us. We were all in therapy. But she was the one out walking dogs every day. She told me that when she was walking the dogs, that was the only time she felt like everything was going to be okay. I said, "Let's all get involved." There we were, a family all walking on the street together or driving a van with our name on it, The Good Shepards. We just had a sense that we were making a difference in this broken world at this very broken time through the pandemic.

We got a phone call from a senior living facility. They said, "We're having a 4th of July event and we need more dogs." At the time we had 75 clients. We decided to call our six best clients and ask if we could keep their dogs for the day and visit the seniors. The dogs' families were absolutely honored to be selected and it was so impactful for the residents. It was very crowded, very unpredictable, and our dogs were perfect.

We were inspired to do more. I contacted a friend who ran a teen group home. They wanted us to bring some dogs and talk to the kids about how we overcame challenges and started a business during the pandemic. We went with seven of our best pups, a more energetic group than we took for the seniors. Isabella shared her story about her learning disabilities, anxiety and depression, about the struggles in our family. She was very transparent about it.

At that event, there was a girl who was very closed off. Head down, not speaking to anyone, isolating herself from the group. Two of the dogs, brothers Elvis and Willie, broke off from the activities we had planned and went over to this girl, Lindsay. They brought their tennis balls and dropped them on her lap and sat with her. Lindsay really opened up to the dogs. Her body language completely changed.

The other kids in the home said, "Lindsay, you're the dog whisperer." Then she came over to the group and started talking with the other kids. The counselors told us afterwards this was her first time opening up and communicating with the rest of the group.

On the way home, Isabella and I were overcome with emotion. I said, this is a movement. This is something that's so needed. This should be a nonprofit. I believe my cluelessness has been my gift—to not know enough to be hesitant or worried about what's next. My approach was: if other people are doing it, why can't I?

As for the inspiration, it was our own lived experience. We know what these dogs have done for us as a family. And when we know more, we should do more. Dogs represent a family of choice—all different shapes and sizes—that come together for a purpose. It's called the pack mentality. A pack is a family. Dogs show a perfect microcosm of how we can move forward together—the resilience, perseverance, utter acceptance, and creativity. In every pack, there's an alpha, a class clown, a reserved dog. Everyone has a role to play. And the dogs are always in the moment.

TAMMEL

What have you learned from equine therapy?

SHEPARD

When I started this nonprofit journey, I looked for other organizations doing what we were doing with a bonded pack of trained dogs. I couldn't find anyone. The existing therapy and service dog organizations we were looking into for guidance didn't quite have the systems we were developing. So I reached out to the equine therapy community. What we're finding is that the way the dogs move together as a single organism reaches the human subject. It's much more like what we're seeing in the equine therapy world in terms of somatic healing, self-regulation, socialization, the exchange of energy. Together the dogs create an organism about the size of a horse.

The equine therapy community has been generous and willing to share information, data, statistics and real measurable outcomes. It's helped us adjust the way we train the dogs and how we approach these encounters.

TAMMEL

How does combining all these disciplines make this unique and powerful?

SHEPARD

It's a combination of our lived experience and really going back and tapping into our own mindsets. I have a test group in my home. We have a pilot program in our family.

When you talk about animal assisted intervention, there's potential for so many different disciplines. We can educate with the animals, partner with them to create healing environments. Our dogs can provide mental health support for vulnerable groups and corporate teams. But they also heal other dogs. We've rehabilitated several shelter dogs from tragic circumstances by integrating them into our well-balanced packs.

Dogs are a bridge to communication, healing, and education. This is proven—being around animals improves cognitive function. My nursing background along with the business experience helps us observe, categorize and learn. We bring it all together and stay really clear on the mission.

TAMMEL

From a business perspective, what does this look like for a corporate wellness program?

SHEPARD

We're developing corporate wellness and team building programs that use the dogs to bring forth concepts like stress relief, conflict resolution, nonverbal communication, and resilience. That's what these dogs do — the power of the pack. Power to heal, power to educate, power to communicate.

Corporate wellness systems can get dry. This brings those

concepts down to a tactile, almost cellular level. It brings us back to nature, back to the way we used to learn.

TAMMEL

What does the model look like and what is the outcome?

SHEPARD

The first session would include pack observation—standing back and observing the dogs socialize with one another, observing the body language. We're observing something, but then we're also going to interpret what we're observing and each one of us will do that from our own lens. It gives us a chance to discuss and include education.

Sometimes it's obedience training, bringing your positive energy. Dogs are predators—that's what's different from equine encounters. Horses are prey animals looking for protection. To get their attention, especially when the power of the pack is in full force, you need to show up as a leader. You need to put your shoulders back and bring a positive, but structured, consistent, authoritative energy. Dogs are looking for strong leadership.

The leadership style is so varied. Everyone can show up as a leader. One's the quiet leader, one's more verbal, one coaxes the group along. To understand yourself in that setting and bring forth that energy—the dogs will feel it.

Our absolute favorite when we work with neurodivergent teens is being a pack leader—putting on a climbing harness, clipping several dogs to your back, and walking in a pack, leading a pack of dogs non-verbally. We've seen it make huge strides in self-expression, confidence building. The ability to understand when to push forward and when to slow down, when to back off. That's the progressive mindset—the ability to work through these obstacles with animals you now have a trusted relationship with.

TAMMEL

What could this look like for a community or society based on what we're learning from the dogs?

SHEPARD

We've gone into the community, corporate spaces, therapeutic spaces, educational spaces. We've seen this elevate the mindset and weave together this togetherness. We need each other, the dogs need each other. We've seen single dogs going into traumatic environments—therapy dogs, service dogs, police dogs—and becoming ill. When the dogs come together, we're better.

Seeking that community—it's so lacking right now. Technology and social media have really stunted our sociability. We have to pull back, get back to our nature. We've seen it work. We know it, we can study it, but we feel it. You can bring your feelings to the corporate space.

You can bring your feelings anywhere. The heightened awareness and resilience it brings has elevated us, has really helped us show up better.

TAMMEL

You've built a model where bonded packs of dogs teach collaboration, shared leadership, and resilience to corporate teams and vulnerable populations. As organizations around the world search for new approaches to wellness and human-centered performance, where do you see this model going beyond Orange County — and what would it look like at a global scale?

SHEPARD

It's interesting how different cultures view the human-animal connection. We have affiliations with trainers and canine businesses in Europe, Latin America, and Canada. We look forward to sharing our programs with like-minded facilitators who share an understanding of the potential for growth.

TAMMEL

You've said you want to share this framework as far and wide as possible. The global leadership development industry is now a $114 billion market, and organizations around the world are searching for approaches like the one you've built. What would it take to bring the Good

Shepards model into organizations and communities across different countries and cultures?

SHEPARD

When I think of global impact that crosses borders and governments, one crisis we need to view this way is human trafficking. We are involved in developing local programs focused on education, trauma recognition, and victims' rights—and moving closer to working with international organizations like A21, a global presence in the anti-trafficking space.

Our bonded packs are ideal for the aftercare programs that are helping to support these survivors as they integrate back into everyday life. When these brave souls don't know which humans to trust again, the dogs are a bridge to that universal language of comfort, confidence, and connection.

TAMMEL

You discovered that single dogs in traumatic environments can become ill, but when the pack comes together, they can sustain more pressure. Organizations around the world face the same challenge — isolated leaders, disengaged teams, and wellness programs that rarely reach people at a cellular level. What does the pack understand about recovery, collaboration, and shared leadership that organizations across the globe still haven't figured out?

SHEPARD

Of course we love all animals, but there's just nothing like a dog—engagement, loyalty, persistence, unconditional love. It's all there in the dog's spirit and an example of how to be a better human. I was recently working with an animal behaviorist who was explaining how wolves were domesticated and therefore became "man's best friend." The wolves with the most social, less aggressive personalities were allowed to stay in the villages and receive protection and share in the hunt. When it comes to dogs, "Survival of the Fittest" is actually "Survival of the Nicest." There is no other species that has sought out human companionship this way—even the evolution of their facial expressions is an example of mirroring the human face.

TAMMEL

How does it feel being a woman at the helm of all this?

SHEPARD

I don't think about it too much because I just am. I've always been a woman. I'm a Mexican American, second generation. I wasn't raised to feel that being a woman was a detriment or that being a woman of color was a detriment. It wasn't until college in the 1980s that I understood the deck may be stacked against me. I just thought everybody had tamales at Christmas.

I was blissfully unaware, just like how I came to the business world, the nonprofit world, even parenting. When I go into a corporate space, it doesn't always occur to me right away that I'm the only woman or the only person of color. The energy I'm bringing, the acumen—even if I was a man, I would still have this specific energy, this unique vision, this different point of view. When I see, feel and hear the dismissal, it is irritating, but there's so many other spaces. I just move to another space. I'm always seeking the confidence to fail spectacularly. Being ready for it, being in acceptance, and being discerning about how far to push and how hard to try and then to move on.

TAMMEL

Where do these powerful mindsets come from?

SHEPARD

I was a daddy's girl. He raised me to see how special I was. I just feel like all of my successes, absolutely my failures, have given me wings, given me another shield, another piece of my coat of armor. All of my experiences being a woman, mothering in the way that I've mothered—I believe every woman is a mother of sorts, a spiritual mother, a world mother. Those experiences and my strong faith have given so many layers and so much depth to my leadership style, my power, my ability to let someone else take the lead.

I've had my ego squashed so many times—it's been great. I'm so thankful for the difficult parts of my story, the grace that I've been given. I feel like there is a mindset to it that is uniquely female. I can't figure out why we're not running the entire world because we should. Leadership is an act of service most of all.

TAMMEL

When you've accomplished everything you dream of, where are you? What does that look like?

SHEPARD

I bought a property in North Orange County, a full acre, an equestrian property. The vision—it's not a matter of if, it's just when—will be a sanctuary and a place for healing, support, celebration and education for vulnerable groups. And also for corporate America, team building, small business, all different types of groups, trauma survivors, youth groups, foster kids.

There will be internships and volunteer opportunities. We'll have a permanent pack of dogs, all from shelters, all with difficult backgrounds, that will come and receive care and rehabilitation and will provide the education and healing. A functioning sanctuary. We'll run programs on the property. We'll also take our programs offsite to corporate settings, churches, parks, schools, colleges. The possibilities are endless.

The dream is to have the facility, buildings and resources to grow this. And to reach out to other organizations and give them the exact framework of what we've done so they can avoid the mistakes we've made and get to where we're going faster. More communities besides ours would have a place like this and understand the potential. To share that and spread out as far and wide as we possibly can.

TAMMEL

What does it mean to you to be a poet and a dreamer?

SHEPARD

A poet is a creative soul, an innovator—someone who creates a kind of music that communicates to others.

My daughter told me,

When I go outside, I put the leashes on the dogs. It's quiet and there's a rhythm to it. The soft tinkling of the collars, the leashes, the metal sound and the clicking of their little feet. I'm walking and it's silent, but it's not silent. There's poetry there.

YOU CAN CHANGE IT...YOU CAN BUILD YOUR OWN

BONNI POMUSH IN CONVERSATION WITH ANNE TAMMEL

Every collection has a conversation that belongs at the end — not because it summarizes what came before, but because it arrives at something the earlier voices were all moving toward without knowing it.

This is that conversation.

Bonni Pomush is CEO of Working Wardrobes and host of the podcast Real Talk, Real Growth. We met through the Orange County leadership community, and I have always admired the way she runs a room — direct, warm, no pretense. When she asked me to come on the podcast, I was the one in the chair for once. Not interviewing. Being interviewed.

I wasn't sure what would come out. What came out was everything. The summer I was sixteen and took my father's advice to do what scares me — knocking on strangers' doors in San Jose, learning I had a gift I least expected. What I learned working for Steve Jobs' publicist that I have never unlearned. Why I left Silicon Valley for Orange County and what I found when I got here. The jazz band model I adopted from Dave Logan's *Tribal Leadership* and Ron McCurdy's Jazz of Leadership at USC. The reason OC CEO Collective exists, and what I am building with Redefining Leadership. The Force Field. The entire architecture.

This conversation closes the book because it is the one where the interviewer finally speaks. Eight women came before me. Andy Cunningham gave me positioning — the architecture that launches everything. Hélène Blanchette shared fourteen countries of cultural intelligence. Van Lai-DuMone reminded me I've come full circle with my mother's great work and intentions. Lacy Schoen gave the movement from inside Fortune 500, where women rise by refusing to disappear. Michèle Fattal shared beauty as leadership architecture. Mikelle Standbridge gave the silence of Italy and the power of stripping away everything that isn't real. Stacie Shepard gave the power of the pack — loyalty as leadership, community as survival. Dita Shemke gave me the last mile, the structure that carries women from qualified to appointed. And Bonni showed me how humans know to grow as flowers — then drew the whole architecture out in a single conversation.

I am grateful to her for asking the right questions. I am grateful to every voice in this book. And I am grateful to you for reading.

BONNI POMUSH

Anne, you started your career at the leading PR and strategy firm in Silicon Valley — led by Steve Jobs' publicist, Andy Cunningham — working on positioning strategy for top tech clients. How did that early work shape how you think today?

ANNE TAMMEL

So much of what I do was shaped by that early beginning. Working for Steve Jobs' publicist, her talent, her tenacity, and her standards were just as high as his. She didn't accept anything less. And honestly, that was a beautiful gift. In the Silicon Valley, especially at Cunningham, if you weren't producing unprecedented outcomes, you didn't belong. You learned very quickly the outcome is absolutely everything.

I've brought that spirit and those standards to every relationship, every challenge, every room I've walked into since.

Probably my most important learning from Steve is:

Everything you see around you — and every environment — was created by someone. A human. No different from you.

If it's not working for you, or if you don't like it, you can change it. You can build your own.

Once you hear that and realize you can apply it — you'll never look at life the same way again.

POMUSH

I love that quote — *you can change it*. That's revolutionary permission. That it doesn't have to stay this way.

TAMMEL

And he proved it. How many of us are on Apple devices?

Andy gave me something that became the foundation for everything I've built. From Andy, I learned that values drive behavior, behavior drives culture, and culture is brand.

That's not a tagline. It's her architecture. And it's the basis for all of my work with strategy and leaders, which I've built on and expanded — it started there, in her offices, watching how positioning at that level truly works.

POMUSH

Growing up in Silicon Valley must have also shaped you. What did that environment give you that you're now bringing, by choice, to Orange County?

TAMMEL

I didn't realize at the time, growing up, that all around me was one of the most culturally integrated societies in the world. We grew up blocks from Japantown with so many cultures thriving all in one space. As kids especially, we didn't know we were different. And there is so much beauty and power in that integration.

That's how Silicon Valley was born — from the way people honor differences, celebrate uniqueness, and bring this to the center of what they're doing.

That's the spirit and the style I bring to Orange County.

POMUSH

We have a tradition here at Real Talk. Real Growth. I love asking about first paycheck stories — because they prove that our careers are never a straight line. What was yours?

TAMMEL

I had just turned sixteen, and I got a summer job walking around knocking on people's doors, inviting them to spend five dollars to get their house number painted on their curb. My mother was aghast. But I took my father's advice:

Do what scares you. Face your fears, conquer them. When you get past them, that's when you really start to develop as a human.

So I was this scared, shy, skinny kid walking around San Jose, knocking on doors. I had no idea how to talk to people. They could have spent the five dollars, or any amount, even one dollar, or they could have slammed the door in my face. Surprisingly, what I found was that most people spent the five dollars. And I started to learn — I had a gift for connecting with people and influencing.

I later found out that not all the numbers actually got painted on the curbs — which I felt terrible about. So this taught me about integrity and authenticity. If you have a gift, you need to use it wisely. And that goes back to Andy Cunningham — discovering your DNA and staying true to it.

POMUSH

You founded OC CEO Collective and SoCal Women in Business. What gap were you seeing in Orange County that made you say — I'm going to build this room myself?

TAMMEL

Coming from Silicon Valley, which was very integrated, to Orange County in my twenties — I was working for Baxter and serving on the board for the American Marketing Association. I'd go to these events and meetings. No one had trained me, nobody taught me how to network. I'd walk into spaces—especially for women—and it was very much a closed circle. You're not this, you're not that. It was a thing.

So I felt like — when you see a need, you almost have to fulfill it. I was at the Park Club talking Chef Pascal Olhats, who ran the top-rated restaurant in Orange County for decades. He said, *Orange County doesn't have a CEO network.*

We used to meet at my restaurant — just to connect as humans. Especially post-pandemic, people need someone who understands them. Who wakes up at night solving the same dilemmas.

So I built this. And the more I've worked with leaders, I've found that women need this the most. We're the most motivated group, because organizations aren't investing in our advancement. We need to invest in ourselves. There's such a need for coming together and empowering one another.

POMUSH

You scaled OC Women in Business by 475% in under three months, and it led to an award-winning event at UCI. What on earth did you do, Anne?

TAMMEL

I drew on my background growing up in San Jose — bringing everyone to the center and uniting them. I threw the greatest party in town and I invited absolutely everyone. And I have learned with women: if I invite them personally, and listen to what matters most, they know they're welcome. And when you invite women into the center to build this with you, it's a completely different picture.

I created this first when I drew on lessons learned from an MFA program where everyone was combative and competitive. I kept saying — *why are we not bringing out the strengths of one another's work and talking about where we can go with it? I was told, Anne, you don't understand how this industry works. There is no collaboration. It's all fighting.*

So I had to create my organization Poets and Dreamers—we started in Orange County and went global with the purpose of *Connecting Continents and Cultures*. Drawing back further, having grown up as the youngest of four sisters, I grew up seeing what happens when powerful women get competitive versus what happens when we come together and celebrate our differences. So I said, *we can do this*. So many people said, *not in that amount of time*. But at three o'clock in the afternoon — after we'd all gotten there at nine — there were two hundred women dancing together.

POMUSH

You've talked about jazz bands and how they inform the best teams. Can you say more about that?

TAMMEL

It all started with the capstone for my first graduate program at USC, the Master of Executive Leadership. I spent an entire semester working on a book called Jazz of Leadership with Ron McCurdy from the Thornton School of Music and Ken Perlman from the Marshall School of Business. The concept was first demonstrated by Dave Logan, author of *Tribal Leadership*.

What Logan discovered is that every organization is made up of tribes that operate at different stages of culture. Some are stuck in dysfunction. Some stay competitive. But at the very highest level, the tribe operates around a shared purpose. No one person dominates, and everyone contributes their unique talent to achieving a shared outcome. This is the space where trust lives and improvisation happens. Where transformation becomes possible.

With his jazz band, McCurdy demonstrates the difference between the outdated hierarchical model where one person at the top dominates, versus our modern flat-level circle where leadership is defined by collaboration. When the band improvises at its highest level, every musician is listening, adapting, and responding as the music gets composed. The spotlight moves. What you're watching is Stage Five tribal culture in real time.

My job that semester was to take *Tribal Leadership* apart, study the each of the stages in the book, then restructure the Jazz manuscript, crafting several of the business sections based on our Friday meetings and integrating everything I knew about leadership, business, and jazz—which I grew up listening to, thanks to my father.

I've adopted what I learned from that into my own practice, which already worked in Silicon Valley strategy, Fortune 100 leadership models, neuroscience from USC's Marshall School, team coaching competencies. From all of this, I'm able to work closely with leaders and in a very short time, explain their organizational dynamics including why they're either working or not working, then pinpoint who's driving the place forward or pulling it back, and write a solid roadmap for how they can get back on track with where they're going—and they often surpass the expectations they first came to me with.

But especially from the Jazz band model, the premise I bring to every environment is that the greatest leader no longer stands at the top. The modern leader builds a dynamic circle of experts. As an example, you excel at something I could never bring. I trust you to perform your best. And we listen to and learn from, rather than talk over and compete with one another.

In business we continuously need to pivot. When we come together as a flat-level circle, we can innovate at a level that top-down organization never could. We each have our solo. And we collectively reach something none could have approached alone.

When I first heard Ron's band play at Stage Five, I called it "approaching the divine."

POMUSH

As for the work you do with executives at major organizations — Google, Citi, YouTube, PwC, Deloitte — what kinds of challenges bring leaders to you? What tends to happen to their trajectory after they work with you?

TAMMEL

I've heard you talk about culture eating strategy for breakfast — and yes that's true. But the real work lies in bringing strategy and culture. It's often an alignment concern. Until a leader truly understands their framework, their strategy, and gives a clear picture of their vision — where they're going in relation to who they are and where they are today — there is no way to convey that and bring the rest of the team along on the journey. Many leadership troubles stem from not knowing how to articulate what you're building.

Once they get that clear picture — here's where we're going, here's what stands in our way, here's what propels us forward, and here's how we'll get there — and then learn how to co-create through having everyone's voices heard and honored, it becomes collaborative. It builds momentum. It becomes a force.

POMUSH

What is it about the way you approach strategy that creates the shift?

TAMMEL

It's coming from a place of authenticity. Who are you truly? What do you bring?

Albert Einstein said the highest form of intelligence is intuition, and I agree with that. But I've recently heard another take on this — that the highest form of intelligence is *metacognition,* the way we think about the way we think. When leaders start looking at their processes and ask — why did I approach it that way? — they build self-awareness. And when a leader adopts self-awareness, it has an enormous effect on their leadership ability.

One quick story: Indra Nooyi, the CEO of Pepsi, would actually stop a meeting if someone was being talked over. She would say, in her very polite, classy, positive way — *Let's hear from her. Let her finish.* She knew that if you let that go and say nothing, you're giving that woman the message: *it's okay for someone to talk over you. You're lucky to be here.* I work with leaders on challenges like that. And the outcome is tremendous.

POMUSH

What do you mean by redefining leadership — by designing a leadership ecosystem — by approaching all of this as a leadership architect?

TAMMEL

I redesign the structure around leaders. Most leadership development focuses on the leader in isolation. You send someone to a program, they come back inspired, then within two weeks the organization has pulled them right back to where they were. Nothing changed around them.

I look at the entire system. Where is the leader relative to their team? What exactly is the culture rewarding? Where is the strategy clear and where is it breaking down? Who on the team is quietly pulling the vision forward and who is lowering the vibe? Then I architect the environment so that when that leader grows, the structure around them supports and accelerates that growth rather than suffocating it.

Force Field is not a coaching conversation. It's a strategic architecture. I map the forces that are propelling a leader or an organization forward — and define the forces blocking them. Then we build the plan, step by step, to accelerate what's working, neutralize what's not, and tap into unseen opportunities while outrunning and sailing past the competition. It draws from Andy Cunningham's positioning methodology, Dave Logan's tribal dynamics, neuroscience research on how the brain changes under pressure, and the decades of working with Fortune 100 leaders across the world to transform teams and organizations.

When you work with enough leaders in a region and they step into their potential collectively, coming together to build a greater community — do you see the model Orange County is becoming? Not just for the nation—but for the world.

Especially for women, we need that space where we can say, *I'm afraid of this, but I'm going to do it anyway.*

POMUSH

You run your organization on several pillars — community, strategy, leadership, and peer advisory. How do these all work together as one system rather than separate offerings?

TAMMEL

They work together because leadership doesn't happen in a vacuum. I designed them as one ecosphere — each element builds the others.

Community is the foundation. Leaders need a space where we can connect as humans. To be seen. To be vulnerable. Not performing — just being present with other leaders who understand the weight of what we're carrying. Without that trust, nothing works.

Peer advisory goes deeper. That's a smaller circle — eight to twelve leaders — where we bring real problems, our greatest fears, and weigh decisions that stand between us and peak performance — or utter failure. It's confidential. It's not competitive.

Especially for women, we need that space where we can say, *I'm afraid of this, but I'm going to do it anyway.* I've watched women — and men — transform in these circles. They walk in carrying something alone then walk out reoriented with an entrepreneurial mindset and powerful strategy. That's life changing.

Strategy is where the architecture happens. That's my Force Field work — positioning, organizational dynamics, building the roadmap. You can have the most supportive community in the world, but if your strategy isn't clear, no team can follow.

Leadership development ties it all together — the self-awareness, metacognition, the jazz band philosophy of improvisational leadership. How you show up. How you listen. How you build cultures where every voice matters.

When all four work together, it's a powerful ecosystem. Leaders grow. Organizations grow, and that ripple effect reaches far beyond any single engagement. That's what I've built. That's the ecosphere.

POMUSH

Before we close — looking back over your career and everything you've seen and done, what would you advise your younger self? And perhaps everyone listening.

TAMMEL

When you have something about you that is very different or very unique — especially when you feel like you just don't fit in — that often turns out to be your superpower.

The same way we build self-aware cultures, if you can stop and ask: *what's unique about me* then honor it, even celebrate it, if over time you can become confident and comfortable in bringing it, communicating it — chances are that's what leads to your greatest contribution.

Sometimes it's about creating the new, unique and different, and doing it in a bold way. Even if it scares you. Sometimes that's your calling. That's your purpose. It's what you need to do in this lifetime.

Imagine when we all bring that. When we all celebrate it. That's where the transformative magic takes place.

WHEN PERSEPHONE SPEAKS
POWER, VOICE, AND THE GLOBAL ARCHITECTURE OF LEADERSHIP

My career began in Silicon Valley then grew in Orange County, advising senior leaders across the globe — work that shaped leadership teams, industries and international markets.

Then I was invited onto larger stages. Offered greater titles. Appointed to lead.

But I learned something that changes everything for women in leadership: we are often appointed to lead and then expected not to lead. To hold the title while others set the direction. To herd and to follow. To be visible — not the visionary.

I dared to lead anyway. Then I discovered what happens when a woman genuinely builds and guides instead of simply performing and maintaining.

I learned what it is like to be a CEO without a board that wants them to succeed. A leader without the infrastructure to match the title. A woman in a room that wants her power and prestige — not her presence.

Research confirms what too many of us have lived: women CEOs are far more likely to be appointed during a crisis and even more likely to be dismissed despite performance. We last an average of 5.2 years compared to 8.1 for men. We are under-sponsored, over-scrutinized, and often the only woman in the room. This takes a psychological, physical, and financial toll that compounds over time. At what price?

For a time, I believed I was alone in this. Then I found other women who had experienced the same. Then I found Persephone.

And I remembered what my father told me: "Women are going to solve this," he would explain. "Women are our true leaders."

In Greek mythology, Persephone was picking flowers in a meadow when Hades discovered her — her visibility, her influence, her momentum — qualities he wanted but did not possess.

So he decided to drag her down with him.

Hades made her Queen. Queen of the Underworld. A throne Persephone never asked for. A kingdom she never chose. A crown without actual power. Presence without a voice.

Persephone was expected to sit. To stay. To be seen and not heard.

She was told this was an honor.

She screamed. No one heard her.

This is not ancient history. And it is not an American story. It is the lived experience of women across 190 economies.

The World Bank's 2026 Women, Business and the Law report measured it: women hold just two-thirds of the legal rights of men worldwide. Not a single economy on earth grants women full economic equality. Only 4% of women live in countries that come close. Laws designed to ensure equal economic opportunity are only half-enforced on average across the world. Safety from violence — the most basic requirement for participation in the economy — is protected by just one-third of the laws that are needed. And those are enforced 20% of the time.

In Sub-Saharan Africa, over 80% of women are self-employed — building businesses from market stalls to tech startups — yet they remain largely locked out of the financial systems that would let them scale. In Pakistan, female bank accounts rose from 20 million to 37 million in four years because one central bank decided to act. In nine of twenty-three middle-income economies, women have reached or are approaching gender parity in startup activity. Rwanda leads the world with women holding 63.8% of parliamentary seats. In Latin America, women hold 36% of parliamentary seats — the highest of any region. Sixty-eight countries passed 113 positive legal reforms for women in the past two years alone. Sub-Saharan Africa led all regions with 33 reforms.

From the outside, it might appear that women in the United States have it all. We own 42% of all businesses. We launched 49% of new businesses in 2024 — the highest share ever recorded. Women-founded startups generate 78 cents of revenue per dollar invested, compared to 31 cents for male-founded startups. We deliver more than twice the return on less than half the capital.

But even in the United States, women-led startups receive barely 2% of venture capital. In Europe, that number is 1%. The International Monetary Fund projects that 40% of global jobs will be disrupted by artificial intelligence — and women hold higher-exposure positions than men in every advanced economy. Fifty-five women now lead Fortune 500 companies — a record — and still just 11% of the total. The gap between what women build and what the system allows us to build is a global condition. Not an American one.

I know this from personal experience. I grew up in Silicon Valley — one of the most culturally integrated societies in the world — and launched my career at the leading communications strategy firm. When I moved to Orange County, I saw the possibility of a region unifying in a way the world had not yet recognized.

California operates as the world's fourth-largest economy. Orange County sits at its center — drawing $2.62 billion in

AI and machine learning venture capital in 2025 alone, with the 2026 Economic Opportunity Report confirming that its most valuable infrastructure is its people. When it does, Orange County is capable of emerging as a global hub for innovation, trade, and strategic leadership.

The challenges women face here — in one of the most advanced innovation economies on earth — are not unlike challenges women face in Nairobi, in São Paulo, in Singapore, in Beirut.

Titles differ. Dynamics do not.

This is the restructuring that sidelines women in leadership. The title without the trust. The seat at the table where her voice is often muted or spoken over. The board that appointed the woman to "lead" but expected her to simply maintain.

These are modern Hades. They do not grab women by the wrist. They do not drag us through a crack in the earth. They do it slowly. Invisibly. Until one day we wake up in kingdoms we never chose, wondering how we landed there.

And here is what every system of silencing knows: our voice is our power. If our voice did not matter, no one would attempt to silence us.

But here is what the mythology does not tell us at first: Persephone did not simply survive the underworld. She stopped waiting to be rescued. She built her own kingdom from the one that tried to bury her.

In fact, when the gods negotiated her release, Persephone could have left the underworld forever. Instead, she ate six pomegranate seeds — binding herself to the darkness.

Some say Hades tricked her. Some say she chose it.

But here is what the seeds truly were: knowledge. Every lesson the underworld taught her. Every power dynamic she learned to read. Every survival skill she forged in the dark.

Persephone did not reject what happened to her. She integrated it.

And when she returned to her throne — the same throne she never asked for — she did not sit as a captive. She sat as a ruler.

Same title. Different woman.

Hades gave Persephone a crown to possess her. She made it real by choosing to rule.

By the end of the story, when Persephone speaks, gods listen. Souls tremble. The underworld obeys.

Hades becomes a footnote in her story.

Persephone became the goddess of both spring and death. She rules two worlds. He rules one basement.

History does not remember Hades as a great king. It remembers him as the man who tried to possess a Queen.

Persephone is not alone in mythology. Inanna — the Sumerian Queen of Heaven — descended through seven gates into the underworld. At each gate, something was stripped from Inanna: her crown, her necklace, her robe, her symbols of power. By the seventh gate, Inanna had nothing. She was hung on a hook. She died.

But Inanna was restored. She ascended back through each gate. She reclaimed everything that had been taken. Inanna emerged more powerful than before.

The pattern is the same across cultures, centuries, and economies:

A woman is recruited for her visibility, her influence, her momentum — then placed where she can be controlled.

That woman is often silenced — her ideas credited to others. Her voice dismissed in meetings. Her strategy overruled by those not capable of building what she builds.

That woman descends into darkness — restructured, sidelined, isolated. Stripped of her authority gate by gate, until she no longer fully recognizes her own voice.

And then — if she understands the pattern, if she returns determined to follow her purpose — that woman rises. Not as a survivor. As a Queen.

We are all surrounded by underworlds. The role that slowly stripped you of your authority — gate by gate — until you no longer recognized your own voice. The workplace that promoted the person who stole your ideas while you were expected to stay silent. The board that appointed you to "lead" and then expected you to simply maintain. The title that came with visibility — not your vision; presence — but not your power.

In Bogotá, a woman builds a technology company then is asked to step aside when the investors arrive. In Lagos, a woman scales a business to hundreds of employees then is denied the loan that would take it further. In Tokyo, a woman leads the strategy then watches a man present it. In Orange County, a woman founds the organization then watches someone else take credit for the very culture she created.

These are modern Hades. The geography changes. The architecture of silencing does not.

So how do we become Queen of the underworld? Persephone shows us.

First: leadership starts within. Demeter raged. The gods intervened. But none could undo what had happened. Persephone was bound to the darkness. No one could save her from having to return. So she stopped waiting to be saved. She learned to rule instead.

The system expects us to wait — for rescue, for validation, for permission. But the only way forward is through mindset. By realizing the power was never outside of us. It always was within.

We do not need permission. We need to recognize the core

power we already have — then build what we need from where we stand.

Second: lessons build leverage. Before Persephone left the underworld, she ate the pomegranate seeds, binding herself to the darkness. But those seeds were knowledge. Experience. Wisdom gained in the underworld — rarely understood by those in the sunlight.

That difficult role taught you boundaries. The workplace that silenced you revealed how inverted power operates — inviting you to build and lead something that cannot be copied and stolen. The board that rejected true leadership sharpened your ability to read and influence rooms. Every setback was preparation. Each challenge built new capability. A spirit of learning builds leverage — if we dare to claim it.

Third: build your own kingdom. Persephone did not return to the underworld as a prisoner. She returned as its rightful Queen. She sat on the throne. She commanded the realm that once captured her.

Your underworld — the system that silenced you, the role that dismissed you, the industry that overlooked you — you do not simply survive. You build from these.

When Persephone was first taken, she screamed, and no one heard her. But by the end of the story, when she speaks, gods listen. Souls tremble. The underworld obeys.

What changed?

Persephone stopped calling out to be rescued. She started speaking to build.

This is the moment we are in. Not just in the United States. Everywhere.

Across 190 economies, women are rising — not because the systems invited us, but because we stopped waiting for invitations. In Sub-Saharan Africa, 33 legal reforms in two years. In Pakistan, 17 million new bank accounts for women in four years. In nine middle-income economies, gender parity in startup activity within reach. In the United States, women are launching half of all new businesses. In Orange County, a region emerging as a global center for innovation and strategic leadership — where the leaders building the architecture are, increasingly, women.

We might look across borders and see only differences. A woman in Nairobi running a market stall and a woman in Newport Beach running a venture fund. A woman in rural Piedmont restoring a monastery and a woman in Singapore leading Fuji Xerox across fourteen countries. A Vietnamese refugee's daughter teaching creativity in corporate boardrooms and a Parisian architect's daughter coaching leaders through visual arts.

Every one of them was told, at some point, that the door was closed.

The differences are real. But the architecture meant to silence was the same. And so is the architecture of rising.

What unites us is not geography. It is the refusal to stay in the kingdoms we were given — and the decision to build our own.

Persephone did not escape the underworld. She learned to rule it. The same crown once meant to contain her became the symbol of her authority. That is the truth every woman eventually discovers: the places designed to silence us become the places that teach us to lead. The underworld is never the end of the story. It is where a woman learns the sound of her own voice — and when she speaks, the world listens.

This book began with Andy Cunningham, who positioned Steve Jobs and built the strategic methodology I learned and continued to build on for twenty-five years. It moved through fourteen countries with Hélène Blanchette. It traveled from a Vietnamese refugee camp to an $8.3 billion industry with Van Lai-DuMone. It entered the sacred spaces of Working Wardrobes with Bonni Pomush, the international blueprint for women rising with Lacy Schoen, the last mile to the boardroom with Dita Shemke, a sixteenth-century monastery in Piedmont with Mikelle Standbridge, the transformative arts of Paris with Michèle Fattal, and the power of the pack with Stacie Shepard.

Ten conversations. Ten leaders. Ten women who refused to stay silent in the rooms they were given.

Innovators. Investors. Strategists. Advisors. Architects. Builders. From Silicon Valley to Orange County to fourteen countries and counting. This is the global movement. This is what the world looks like when women come together — not waiting to be invited, but building the stage, the strategy, and the future.

Uniting and empowering women worldwide.

The poets and the dreamers aren't waiting for the world to be ready.

They're building it.

AFTERWORD

Leaders, more than ever, are building across borders. Across every industry, every stage of business, every economy on earth.

This book began as a series of conversations — some recorded at The Park Club in Costa Mesa, some across continents, all between leaders who chose to speak with the honesty that only comes when you know you are being heard.

The women in these pages positioned the most iconic technology brands of our era, led organizations across fourteen countries, built an $8.3 billion industry from nothing but innate strengths, transformed a nonprofit from a 2.3 to a 4.3 on Glassdoor in two years, designed an international leadership blueprint, built the structure that carries women from qualified to appointed, restored a sixteenth-century monastery into a global artist residency, coached leaders through the creative arts in Paris, and modeled the power of the pack for the world.

What connects us is not gender. It is the refusal to accept that the rooms we entered were the rooms we needed to stay in. We built new spaces.

Poets and Dreamers: Global Icons and Innovators belongs to a series. The larger collection, *Poets and Dreamers: Thought Leaders and Visionaries,* spans seventeen interviews — Silicon Valley pioneers, neuroscientists, jazz musicians, young inventors, global strategists, and some of the women you have just met in these pages.

The poets and dreamers are waiting.

For the full collection, look for Poets and Dreamers: Thought Leaders and Visionaries, soon to be available wherever books are sold.

ABOUT THE AUTHOR

Anne Tammel is a Fortune 100 strategy advisor to leaders at Google, YouTube, PwC, Citi, Deloitte, Ernst & Young, and IBM. A Silicon Valley native, Anne began her career bringing innovation to market at Cunningham Communication — the firm that positioned Steve Jobs, launched the Macintosh, and represented the defining technology leaders of its era — then spent 25 years developing proprietary frameworks for leaders to position and scale peak-performing global organizations.

Founder of OC CEO Collective and SoCal Women in Business, Anne's advisory work spans $15 billion in enterprise value across Fortune 100 corporations, global enterprises, and emerging ventures. Her Redefining Leadership architecture bridges high-level business strategy and human-centric leadership.

Author of the Redefining Leadership Series (International Leadership Press), Anne's collection *Poets and Dreamers: Thought Leaders and Visionaries* debuted in limited scope as the #1 Bestselling New Release in Interviews. Having advised C-suite executives, global teams, and Olympic champions, she holds an Executive Master of Leadership,

USC Sol Price School of Public Policy; an MBA, USC Marshall School of Business; and PCC (executive coaching) and ACTC (team coaching) credentials from the International Coaching Federation. She integrates systems thinking, emotional intelligence, and neuroscience into her work.

Recognized by CBS Los Angeles for leading community transformation, Anne leads the regional movement redefining leadership, redesigning organizational culture, and advancing women in business since 2001.

instagram.com/annetammel

facebook.com/annetammel

YOUR LEGACY, OUR STRATEGY
CEO COLLECTIVE

Step into the circle.

The higher we rise as leaders, the fewer spaces we have to speak authentically about the decisions that define us.

CEO Collective Peer Advisory Circles are confidential, high-trust forums for founders, CEOs, and senior executives navigating high-stakes decisions across growth and scale.

Each circle is curated by industry, revenue stage, and leadership focus—bringing together leaders working through decisions across growth, capital, leadership, and culture.

This is executive-level advisory, grounded in real-time decisions.

Bring the challenges that matter most.

Leave with clarity, aligned perspective, and a strategic path forward.

 *This is the room I wish I had ten years ago.*

You are invited to join CEO Collective for a private Peer Advisory Session, held in person or online. Circles are curated by invitation.

Reserve your seat.

Scan to Join the CEO Collective

Facilitated by OC CEO Collective

Strategic advisors to global leadership teams

ALSO BY ANNE TAMMEL

Poets and Dreamers: Thought Leaders and Visionaries

Redefining Leadership™ *(forthcoming)*